She had no idea what he would do....

"Shirts on the left, sweaters on the right," Jessica decided as she began to fold and stack. Her hand touched something hard in the pocket of one of Mike's shirts. Jessica reached in, expecting to find some car part he had forgotten about.

But it wasn't. Jessica stared at the black metal object in her hand, hardly able to believe her eyes. She felt a thrill of fear race up her spine. *And where does the gun go?* she wondered numbly. *On the left or the right?*

For a few minutes Jessica just sat there, staring at the gun in her hand, too numb to move or to think. Mike had a gun. What for? Why hadn't he told her? Mike, a man with the temper of a neutron bomb, had a gun. Had he ever used it? Would he ever use it? Would he ever use it on her?

Suddenly, like a dam exploding, Jessica started to cry. All the tension and strain and fear of the past weeks came down on her at once. She'd fallen in love with Mike, and she'd thought that meant that she knew him. But she didn't know him. She had no idea who he was, no idea what he would do.

Bantam Books in the Sweet Valley University series:

SWEET VALLEY UNIVERSITY™

A Married Woman

Written by
Laurie John

Created by
FRANCINE PASCAL

BANTAM BOOKS
NEW YORK · TORONTO · LONDON · SYDNEY · AUCKLAND

A MARRIED WOMAN
A BANTAM BOOK 0 553 40821 6

Originally published in USA by Bantam Books

First publication in Great Britain

PRINTING HISTORY
Bantam edition published 1995

Conceived by Francine Pascal

Produced by Daniel Weiss Associates, Inc,
33 West 17th Street, New York, NY 10011

Bantam Books are published by Transworld Publishers Ltd,
61–63 Uxbridge Road, Ealing, London W5 5SA,
in Australia by Transworld Publishers (Australia) Pty Ltd,
15–25 Helles Avenue, Moorebank, NSW 2170,
and in New Zealand by Transworld Publishers (NZ) Ltd,
3 William Pickering Drive, Albany, Auckland.

Printed and bound in Great Britain by
Cox & Wyman Ltd, Reading, Berkshire.

For Alice Elizabeth Wenk

Chapter One

Elizabeth Wakefield was having a dream. In the dream, her twin sister, Jessica, was standing on top of a wedding cake as big as an apartment building. Instead of a white bridal dress and veil, she was wearing jeans and a motorcycle helmet. Instead of a handsome groom in a black morning coat and pinstripe trousers standing proudly beside her, there was nothing beside her but empty space. The only traditional thing about the scene was the enormous bouquet of flowers in Jessica's arms, but the flowers had all been crumpled and broken. Jessica was crying.

Elizabeth was standing at the foot of the cake, shouting up at Jessica, trying to make herself heard over her sister's heartbroken sobs. "Throw the bouquet!" Elizabeth was screaming. "Throw the bouquet, Jess; then everything will be all right. Throw the bou-

1

quet, and then you can come down. Throw it!"

"But you have to catch it, Elizabeth!" Jessica shouted back. "If you don't catch it, I can never come down."

Elizabeth felt hot tears fill her own blue-green eyes. "I'll catch it!" she shouted. "I promise I will."

Trembling and half-blind with crying, Jessica slowly raised the flowers over her head. "Please catch this," she repeated. "If you catch the bouquet, then I can come down. Then everything will be all right."

Elizabeth's eyes were fixed on the clump of pink, white, and yellow flowers and the slender, shivering figure on top of the cake. She held out her arms, ready, but as Jessica hurled the bouquet into the air the flowers flew apart, showering down, so that trying to catch them was like trying to catch raindrops.

"I told you!" Jessica wailed. "I told you . . . I told you . . ."

Elizabeth woke with a start. Still half in her dream, she blinked in the early-morning light. *Where am I?* she wondered, suddenly aware that she wasn't in her bed in the dorm, but on the sofa of an unfamiliar room. She sat up, her eyes moving from the wooden blinds to the wall of books and CDs, to the broken flowers scattered all over the floor, just like the ones in her dream.

"Jessica," Elizabeth whispered aloud as the

terrible events of the night before came back to her in a rush. How could she have forgotten even for one second?

Yesterday—Saturday—had been the main day of Sweet Valley University's Parents' Weekend. Mr. and Mrs. Wakefield had come down to the campus for the first time since the beginning of the term, eager to see their twin daughters after so long a separation.

Unfortunately, one of their twin daughters had been less than eager to see them. Jessica had secretly moved in with her boyfriend, Mike McAllery, a few weeks before and was trying to keep her parents from finding out. Not that Elizabeth could blame Jessica. Their parents would have been upset by the idea of their daughter moving in with any man, and devastated if they knew it was Mike McAllery.

Mr. and Mrs. Wakefield would only need to take one look at Mike McAllery to realize that he was no good. He was a twenty-two-year-old biker, demonically handsome, with lots of money and a bad attitude.

And to make matters worse, Mike adored Jessica and was demanding to meet Mr. and Mrs. Wakefield at the first possible opportunity.

Jessica had plotted and schemed to keep her parents and Mike separate this weekend. She'd lied to her parents, telling them she had no boyfriend at all, and lied to Mike, telling him her parents wouldn't be coming for the weekend. And not for the first time, one of Jessica's schemes hadn't turned out exactly the way she'd planned. Last night the entire Wakefield family was piled into the Jeep on their way to dinner when Mike McAllery had passed them in his '64 Corvette, shattering at least one part of Jessica's charade.

Elizabeth shuddered and pulled the blanket more tightly around her, though she wasn't really cold. It was the memory of Mike Mc-Allery's face, the hard, gold eyes staring at Jessica as though he'd caught her with another man, that made Elizabeth shake. Jealous, resentful, and used to his own way, Mike McAllery was obviously a man with a temper whom you didn't want to cross.

Her eyes scanned the room again. Jessica had witnessed Mike McAllery's temper last night. The floor was strewn not only with damaged flowers but with tipped-over furniture, magazines, and broken pieces of glass. The only thing that wasn't damaged—physically at least—was Jessica herself.

When Elizabeth arrived on the scene, the apartment door had been wide open and Jessica, exhausted with crying, had been clinging to the side of the bed, terrified that Mike might come back and try to hurt her.

Elizabeth got up from the sofa slowly and

went into the kitchen to make some coffee. She could only imagine what her parents must be thinking. First Jessica had fled the restaurant before dessert, and then Elizabeth had abruptly left the dance and never come back.

She filled the espresso maker with water, but she was still thinking about Jessica, crouched beside the bed in fear. Last night Elizabeth had left her mother sitting by herself at the dance because she'd suddenly realized something important. Something that had been staring her in the face but that she'd been unable to see. For weeks now Elizabeth had been trying to discover the identity of the man who ran the violent and openly racist secret society on campus, but he constantly eluded her. Last night, though, as she remembered Mike McAllery's face in the car, everything had fallen into place. Her own sister was living with the leader of the secret society. Elizabeth felt sure of it.

She poured out two cups of the hot, fragrant liquid and put them on a small lacquer tray. It wasn't until she had arrived here last night, wanting to warn Jessica about Mike, that Elizabeth learned the frightening truth.

Jessica was more powerfully tied to Mike McAllery than Elizabeth had ever imagined: he wasn't just Jessica's boyfriend, he was her husband.

Elizabeth closed her eyes, wishing that, too,

had been part of her dream last night. But she knew it wasn't. It was real.

Elizabeth crossed into the bedroom. The blinds were partially open, illuminating the photographs of dead blues musicians and old motorcycles on the pearl-gray walls and the slender body huddled on one side of the king-size bed, her golden hair spilling across the black pillow like sunlight.

"Jess," Elizabeth said softly. "I made some coffee."

The sea-green eyes opened instantly. Jessica sat up slowly, her expression serious. "Thanks," she said. "I wasn't really sleeping. I was just . . . you know . . . Thinking."

Elizabeth sat on the edge of the bed, carefully setting the tray beside her. "I've been thinking, too," she said. "You can't stay here, Jess. Maybe you should go back home for a little while."

"Go back home?" Jessica's expression was as horrified as her voice. "What about midterms? What about Mike?"

What about Mike? Elizabeth thought. "Please at least move out of here," she said aloud. "Move back in with Isabella, Jess. Get some space."

Coffee spilled over the side of the cup as Jessica raised it to her lips. "I can't," she said. "Mike is my husband." She smiled, but Elizabeth could see that it was forced. "We're having problems, Elizabeth, that's all. We'll work them out." She put her cup back down, forcing the smile even harder. "All newlyweds have problems."

Elizabeth leaned forward, touching her sister's hand. "Jessica," she said urgently, "listen to me, please. You and Mike aren't having normal newlywed problems. The man is violent, jealous, possessive—"

Jessica put her hands to her ears. "Stop it, Elizabeth. I know you don't like Mike, but you don't know him. He isn't at all what you think he is. He's sweet and kind. He loves me."

Elizabeth had resolved to be gentle with Jessica, but that resolve was swiftly slipping away. "Sweet and kind men don't beat up the women they love."

"But he didn't beat me up," Jessica countered. "He told me to run away so that he wouldn't."

"Oh, pardon me," Elizabeth said. "I guess that makes him a saint."

Jessica ignored her sarcasm, her eyes on the tray. "I want you to go before he gets back, Elizabeth," she said at last. She raised her eyes to her twin's. "This is my problem, and I'm the one who has to solve it."

Elizabeth could only stare at her sister in surprise—surprise and with a flicker of grudging respect. This was the first time in eighteen years that Jessica Wakefield had ever accepted responsibility for anything.

"You don't have to stay here," Elizabeth said, choosing her words carefully. "Maybe if you and Mike just take a little time away from each other—"

But Jessica's head was shaking again. "I'm a married woman now, not a little girl. This time I'm not running away."

"What is it with the women in my family?" Steven Wakefield asked aloud as he banged the receiver of the phone back down. "Why don't they ever do what they're supposed to?"

Billie, his girlfriend, looked up from the pancake batter she was stirring. "Does this mean Elizabeth hasn't gone back to the dorm yet?"

Steven leaned against the kitchen counter with a sigh. "Where could she be, Billie? It's not like Elizabeth to stay out all night." He glanced at the clock on the stove. "My parents are going to arrive any minute. They're going to think it's pretty weird if neither of their daughters is here to say good-bye to them."

"You should have thought of that before you invited them to brunch when neither of your sisters was around to say whether she could make it or not," Billie said. "And anyway, they're not going to think it's all that weird."

8

She put the bowl of batter aside. "What's weird is the fact that both their daughters disappeared last night without much of an explanation." She plugged in the coffeemaker, giving him a mischievous smile. "Although after getting stuck with William White for nearly half an hour, your mother may have her own ideas about why Elizabeth took off like that," she added.

Steven gazed back at her, puzzled. William White was sophisticated, intelligent, polite, and from one of the oldest and wealthiest families in the country, yet Billie and his mother had taken a dislike to him at the first hello.

"What's wrong with William?" Steven asked. "He seems okay to me."

Billie smirked. "You mean he isn't Mike McAllery, so he's got to be all right."

Steven scowled. No matter how hard he tried, he would never get over the fact that someone as sensible, practical, and levelheaded as Billie insisted on defending a piece of scum like Mike McAllery. "No, he isn't Mike McAllery," he said irritably.

Billie shrugged. "William is like virtual reality man." She ducked into the refrigerator and came out with a bowl of fruit salad and a platter of cheese. "You know, too good to be true."

Steven took the dishes from her hands. "And Mike McAllery's too terrible *not* to be true." He looked down at the floor, as though he could see through the linoleum and wood to the apartment below. "Do you think I should go get Jess?" he asked. "I mean, it's not like she'd have to come far. You would think she could tear herself away from loverboy for an hour or two. That's not asking so much."

Billie started getting the plates out of the cabinet. "I think I'd forget about Jess," she said. "The way she raced away from the restaurant last night, I think there might be a little trouble in paradise."

For the first time in days Steven's face lit up with a spontaneous smile. "Really?"

"Yeah, really," Billie said. "I have a hunch Jessica's beginning to realize that she's in a little over her head."

Steven's smile grew. It was the first good news he'd heard since his sister had moved into the apartment below several weeks before. He'd been right not to tell his parents. Everything was going to work itself out.

Billie gave him a look. "What are you grinning about?" she asked. "It's not over yet, you know."

"No," he said, "but I know Jessica Wakefield. If she and Mike are having problems, she'll be out of there before he can ask her where she put his razor. Steadfast is not Jessica's middle name."

Billie started setting the plates on the table.

"You'd better think of some reason for Elizabeth's absence this morning or stupid will be yours."

Celine Boudreaux rolled over with a groan. After the dance last night, she'd gone for a drive with Peter Wilbourne and they'd wound up in a secluded spot by the beach, making out in the back of his car. Now her face felt as though she'd spent most of the evening rubbing sandpaper over it.

"Men," Celine muttered, squinting as she opened her eyes even though the blinds were tightly shut. "My granny was right. Living with them is harder than living without them."

She touched her face, but she was no longer thinking of Peter; she was thinking instead of Tom Watts. Tom had been cold and standoffish toward her during the first few months of the school year, but recently he'd been showing interest. They'd been out on a couple of dates, but so far he had resisted kissing her. No man had ever resisted kissing Celine for more than one date. Yet in a way that was part of Tom's charm.

"What about you, Princess?" Celine asked, addressing her question to Elizabeth's bed. "Has Tom Watts kissed you? Does he kiss better than William? Does he make your knees go weak?"

Celine waited for Elizabeth's reply, but none

came. If Little Miss Dull-but-Perfect was still asleep, she must have gotten in even later than Celine thought.

"What'd you and William do last night?" Celine drawled, propping herself up on one elbow. "Go all the way?" The taunting smile locked on her lips.

Elizabeth's bed was not only empty, it hadn't been slept in. Celine whistled. "Well, well, well," she said softly. "Don't tell me William really has conquered Elizabeth the Pure after all."

She reached for the cigarettes and matches on the table by her bed. The thought of William making love to Elizabeth caused a white-hot rush of jealousy to flood her heart, but she forced it away. "Don't be silly," she chided herself. "William's attracted to Elizabeth the way a boa constrictor's attracted to a mouse." She lit a cigarette, exhaling through a slow smile. "In the end, he's going to eat her alive."

Celine was still comforting herself with the image of the wreck Elizabeth would be when William White was through with her when there was a knock on the door.

"What's the matter, sugar, forget your keys?" Celine muttered to herself as she slithered from the bed.

Celine pulled open the door, just managing to swallow her exclamation of surprise. "Why, William," she said, putting on one of her bored faces, "to what do I owe this early-morning honor?"

"To nothing," he said, staring over her head. "Where's Elizabeth? Did she go out already?"

What to do, what to do, Celine chanted to herself as she smiled at him dumbly. *Cover for Elizabeth or tell the truth?*

He pushed past her in his arrogant, it's-my-world way. "Well?" he demanded. "Where is she? Is she meeting her parents for breakfast somewhere?"

Tell the truth, Celine decided. *That was the right and moral thing to do.*

"Don't tell me you lost her," Celine said in mock horror.

William took one of her cigarettes and sat down on Elizabeth's bed, lighting the cigarette with a flick of his finger. "What are you talking about, *lost her?*" he practically snarled. "Where is she?"

Celine's pretty face was drawn with concern. "Why, William," she said, "I thought she must be with you."

"Yeah, thanks," Tom was saying. "No, I don't want to leave a message. Yeah, I'll try again later." For the third time that morning he hung up the phone on his desk and sat back, staring at the screen of his computer.

Where was Elizabeth? Last night she'd come

to his room looking for him. He'd held his breath while she stood outside, knocking and calling. "I have to talk to you," she'd said. "It's about the story. I think I found something."

But Tom hadn't answered the door. He'd sat there, the box that contained all that was left of the old Tom Watts on the desk before him, willing her away. *Go away!* he'd silently screamed. *I don't want you to see what I was. I don't want you any closer than you are.* She'd stayed out there for so long, calling to him, that he'd almost feared she knew he was there. Finally she'd gone. He'd heard her footsteps hurry down the hall, and he'd even peered through the curtains and watched her run across the parking lot to her Jeep, blond hair flying behind her, jump into the driver's seat, and gun the engine so hard that the vehicle squealed onto the road. Almost instantly he'd wished that he'd answered the door. *Are you totally nuts?* he'd railed at himself. *What if she really has found out something about the society? What if she decides to face them alone?* In the end he'd finally managed to catch a few fitful hours of sleep by convincing himself that Elizabeth wasn't stupid enough to do something that dangerous. Now, however, he wasn't so sure.

Tom chewed his bottom lip, his eyes staring blindly at the screen. Where did Elizabeth go last night? He'd been calling her dorm since

14

eight in the morning, but she wasn't there. He'd tried to tell himself that she might have stayed with her parents at their hotel, but she didn't tear out of the parking lot like that to join her parents for a quiet family evening.

Shoving the computer mouse away from him, Tom tilted back his chair. If anything happened to Elizabeth, he had only himself to blame. He should have answered the door last night—if he were honest, he would have answered it the second he heard her call his name—but he couldn't. Nailed into the night by the past, he couldn't have spoken, couldn't have moved.

And now he had a real problem. There was one person who might know where Elizabeth was: Celine. And Celine was the last person on the planet Tom felt like dealing with now. He'd been courting Celine lately because his instincts told him she could lead him to the mastermind of the secret society, but as jobs went he'd rather be shoveling out the elephant house at the zoo. Every time she sidled up to him with her kiss-me-now mouth and her come-over-here eyes, he felt like shouting and running away.

"I can't face her this morning," he told the computer. "I just can't. I hardly slept at all last night."

Elizabeth's voice called out to him in his

15

mind. "Tom, I've got to talk to you. I found out something about the story."

What had she found out? And who else knew?

Leaving the computer on, Tom grabbed his jacket and left the studio, running across the campus the way he used to run across the football field: gracefully, easily, quick as a cat.

Celine was almost dressed in a pair of red stretch pants and a gauzy see-through tunic in shades of pink. Her face was so made up, her hair so beautifully tousled, that he almost thought she'd known he was coming.

"Why, sugar," Celine purred as she opened the door to him. "What a pleasant surprise. Don't tell me you've come to take me to brunch."

Tom stared at her, knowing for certain how the next few hours of his life would be spent: watching Celine eat something expensive and exotic while her foot stroked his ankle under the table. He'd rather be having his cavities drilled.

"It's such a beautiful morning, I couldn't stand the thought of being stuck in the studio when I could be out with you," he lied.

She kissed his cheek, leaving, he knew, her lips imprinted in red. "Just give me five minutes and I'll be ready," she promised.

He kept his back to her while she changed from the outfit she was wearing into the outfit she was going to wear.

16

"Elizabeth out with her parents already?" he asked over his shoulder, hoping he sounded disinterested enough.

Celine laughed. "Out with her parents? You are an idealist, aren't you?" Tom usually loved a woman's laugh. Elizabeth's sounded like silver bells to him, but Celine's always reminded him of panic-stricken bats. "Sugar, Elizabeth hasn't come back from last night."

Tom knew what Celine was insinuating in her sly, unsubtle way. She was insinuating that Elizabeth was with a man. Tom stared at Elizabeth's neatly made bed. As sick as the thought made him feel, he couldn't help hoping it was true.

Isabella was feeling a little bit like Alice in Wonderland this morning. Twenty-four hours ago she'd been convinced that Tom Watts was the man for her. For weeks, even months, she'd carried a small but steady torch for him, and he hadn't given her as much as a second glance. And then she'd become friends with Danny Wyatt, Tom's roommate. Danny and Isabella had schemed and plotted to get her and Tom together. Somehow, though, the more time she spent with Danny, the closer they became. Last night was supposed to be their last great offensive against Tom, but Tom, as usual, had been too busy to show up for it. And then, somewhere between the movie and the pineapple pizza afterward, Isabella and Danny had forgotten about Tom completely and admitted that they were falling in love with each other. Now here they were, after a night of nonstop talking, having their first official brunch as a couple in the campus coffeehouse.

"I don't believe this," Isabella suddenly said, putting down her cappuccino with a thud. "I thought Tom couldn't come with us last night because he had so much work to do." She gave Danny an affectionate smile. "Not that I'm not grateful to him for staying in the studio," she went on. "If he'd come with us, I might never have realized I was chasing the wrong man, but I still can't believe he's started dating creatures of the night."

Danny, busy sliding half of his omelette onto Isabella's plate and half of her feta-and-spinach crepes onto his, didn't bother to look over his shoulder. "Celine?"

Isabella speared one of his home fries with her fork. "Known to those who love her best as the Wicked Witch of the West." She set down her fork and caught his hand between hers. "It's lucky I found the man of my dreams or I might be insulted that Tom's always been oblivious to my charms but doesn't mind being seen in public with her. A girl could get a complex about a thing like that."

"Don't take it personally," Danny said with a

laugh. "Tom can't stand Celine. If he and Celine were the last two people left on earth, he'd demand a recount."

The café was crowded and understaffed this morning, so Tom and Celine had to wait by the door for a free table. Isabella studied them while Danny divided their meals. Celine was tossing her thick mane of honey-blond hair and gushing on as usual, her syrupy voice rising about the general din of the café and her full skirt swaying even though she was standing still. Tom stood beside her, looking somehow as though he owned the place, one hand on Celine's elbow, not so much with her as showing her off. He didn't look like a man who was suffering. If what Danny said was true, Tom was a pretty good actor.

"Then why is he out with her?" Isabella asked. "And why is he acting so macho and self-important? I've never seen Tom like this before."

Danny glanced over his shoulder. "To answer your second question, that's Wildman Watts you're seeing strutting up there," he said, turning back before his eyes met Tom's. "The best college quarterback in the history of the state. He isn't around much anymore, but I guess Celine's the kind of girl to bring him out of retirement." He set Isabella's plate back in front of her. "And to answer your first question, I

don't know what Tom's up to, but he's definitely going through one of his intense phases."
Danny picked up his glass of juice. "He won't
tell me much about the story he's working on
now, but whatever it is, it must be heavy. He's
even moodier and more remote than usual."

Isabella helped herself to another home fry.
"You think that's why he's hanging out with
Celine and acting weird? Because of this story?"

Danny nodded. "Believe me, Iz, it's the only
possible reason."

She chewed thoughtfully. "Unless she's
blackmailing him . . ."

Danny looked at her sharply. "Blackmailing
Tom? I know I said he's a little secretive, but
that doesn't mean he's ripe for blackmail."

Isabella brought her eyes away from Tom
and Celine. All at once she had the feeling that
Danny knew some things about Tom Watts that
no one else did. "I was only joking," she said
quickly.

Across the room, Celine Boudreaux laughed.

"I'm really sorry you had to wait so long,"
the waitress was saying as she cleared away their
empty dishes, "but one of the girls who's supposed to be on this shift with me called in sick
this morning and the other hasn't turned up
yet, so I'm doing three sets of tables."

Winston was listening with only one ear. His

other ear was listening to the conversation his mother was having with Denise Waters. His mother finished her story of the time Winston made chocolate popcorn and nearly totaled the kitchen and switched abruptly to the subject of children. In fact, unless the strain of the weekend was distorting Winston's hearing, his mother seemed to be asking Denise how many children she planned to have.

"Mom . . ." Winston moaned, trying not to blush. "Come on. We're not married, you know."

Denise laughed. "I think it's a little early to be thinking about children," she said.

"That's what everyone says," Mrs. Egbert informed her, "but these things sneak up on you." She turned to her husband. "Don't they?"

Mr. Egbert seemed more concerned with the bill sneaking up on them. "Um," he said, not raising his eyes from the rectangle of paper.

"That's how we had Winston," she went on blithely. "He snuck up on us."

Winston could feel himself losing the battle of the blush. "Mom, I'm begging you . . ."

Denise slid one slender arm around his shoulders. It was like being enveloped in sunlight. "He sort of snuck up on me, too," she said, giving him a squeeze.

Winston had to stop himself from sliding to the floor. He'd been prepared for the fact that his mother would spend the weekend

21

embarrassing him by telling Denise stories about all the dumb things he did when he was a little kid, but he hadn't been prepared for Denise's acting talents. She was giving an Oscar-winning performance by anybody's standards.

"I'm going up front to pay," Mr. Egbert announced, getting to his feet. "That girl won't be back here till Christmas, the rate she's going."

As soon he was out of hearing Mrs. Egbert reached out and patted Denise's hand. "I just want you to know how happy meeting you has made me and Mr. Egbert," she said. "We were a little worried when Winston told us he was living in a girls' dorm. At least Mr. Egbert was. I tried to tell him it was just the sort of thing that happens to Winston, but he didn't take much comfort in that."

Winston looked down at his watch. Five minutes, ten at the most, and his parents would be on their way back home. All he had to do was survive it. "I think Dad's ready," he said, jumping to his feet so quickly that he knocked over an empty water glass. "We'd better go."

Mrs. Egbert sighed. "I guess he'll always be clumsy," she said. "I used to think he'd grow out of it, but I've just about given up now."

Denise linked one arm through Winston's and one through his mother's as they left the coffeehouse. "You've raised the most wonderful

22

son," she said, laughing. "But I do try to keep anything breakable out of his way."

Denise's arm was still through Winston's as they watched his parents pull out of the parking lot. They both waved with their free hand. Mrs. Egbert turned in the passenger seat, waving and blowing a kiss, and his father tooted the horn.

"We did it," Winston whispered as the black sedan turned the corner and disappeared. "We fooled them."

Denise hugged him. "We were brilliant, if I do say so myself," she said. "They really believed that I'm your girlfriend."

Just in time, Winston stopped himself from hugging her back. He'd almost believed it, too.

"I can't help it if I'm sick," Jessica said, her voice tight and slightly choked.

Artie Stigman, the manager of the campus coffeehouse, laughed humorlessly. "Isn't it funny how often you get sick on sunny weekends? You ever think of getting sick on a rainy Wednesday, Jess? Or on an overcast Thursday afternoon when there are only six people in the place and they're all just drinking coffee?"

"But I am sick," Jessica wailed. "You wouldn't want me to infect everyone, would you?"

Artie sighed heavily. "It's Sunday and half the freshmen parents are still here, Jess," he said. "The place is packed, Molly broke her wrist doing the twist at that dance last night, and my grill chef has a hangover. You may be the worst waitress I've got, you may very well be the worst waitress in the whole state of California, but today I need you. I don't care if you have smallpox as long as the rash isn't on your face and hands."

"But I have a fever," Jessica argued. "I'm burning up."

"Take some aspirin and get your butt over here in the next ten minutes, Jess, or you're going to have a long convalescence."

Jessica's grip tightened on the telephone. "What does that mean? Are you threatening me?"

"I'm not threatening you," Artie said, shouting slightly over the sound of someone dropping a tray of china. "I'm telling you. If you don't get here pretty damn fast, you don't have to bother getting here ever again. Am I making myself clear?"

"You're firing me?"

"Think of it more like you're quitting."

"All right, fine! I quit!" she screamed. She slammed down the phone and threw herself across the bed, her face in the already-damp pillow.

"I don't care," she sobbed as the impact of this new disaster rolled over her. "I don't care. What does anything matter now?"

She'd been waiting all morning for Mike to come back, sitting on the edge of the bed as though she were carved from wood, counting the minutes, jumping every time she heard a motorcycle outside or someone coming up the stairs. She'd been so intent on listening for Mike that she was already an hour late for her shift before she remembered she was supposed to work today.

She sat up, reaching to the bedside table for a tissue to blow her nose. Next to the tissues was the photograph of them the night they got married, at the diner where they'd had their wedding feast. The owner had taken it. She and Mike were standing together in front of the jukebox, arms entwined. They looked like a couple in an ad for jeans—Mike so darkly handsome and dangerous looking, Jessica the perfect California blonde—but more than that, they looked happy. You only had to notice the way his hand fell on her shoulder, the way her head leaned against his chest, to know they were in love. Madly, passionately in love.

Jessica reached for another tissue as fresh tears streamed down her cheeks. How could it all have gone so wrong so quickly?

She loved Mike, she really did—she'd never loved anyone like this before, not even in her imagination. Why couldn't they make it work?

Why did they keep pushing each other closer and closer to the edge?

There was the roar of a 1000-cc engine in the parking lot below. Jessica froze, her heart suddenly pounding so hard and so loudly that she thought it might explode. As much as she wanted the nightmare of waiting to be over, to be back in Mike's arms, she was afraid. Every time they had a fight, he was just that little bit more angry and more violent than the time before. He loved her—Jessica knew he loved her—but she was beginning to realize that didn't mean he wouldn't hurt her.

The front door opened with a bang. Jessica turned to the door, not daring to breathe.

He hadn't slept either. There were circles under his eyes and his face was dark with stubble. It looked like he'd taken a fall on the bike, because there was a gash in his jacket and his jeans were covered with mud.

The thousand things Jessica had planned to say to him stampeded through her mind. How sorry she was. How childish she'd been. How much he'd scared her. How she was trying her best, she really was. She couldn't say any of them, though; there were too many tears blocking her words.

Mike didn't speak. He stood in the doorway for a few seconds, staring at her silently, his own eyes glistening with tears, and then he came over to the side of the bed and knelt down, his head on her lap.

"Take me back," he whispered. "Please, baby. Take me back."

Chapter Two

"Married? Jessica? *What?*"

Nina Harper dropped the carton she was holding and orange juice splattered across the desk. They were having breakfast in Nina's room because Elizabeth didn't want to risk anyone else's overhearing the news about her twin. "Your sister's married?" Nina grabbed a napkin and wiped up the juice. "You're kidding, right?" she asked when she had composed herself. "This is some kind of joke."

"I wish it were," Elizabeth said. She took another small bite of toast, but she didn't feel like eating. That should have been a relief. Elizabeth had been so unhappy in the beginning of the semester, she'd drowned her sorrows in junk food and put on weight. But now, slowly, she was losing it. Maybe she'd discovered the perfect diet at last: the Your-Sister-Is-Married-to-a-Violent-Criminal diet.

Nina, however, was smiling warily. "Are you sure you're not misunderstanding this somehow?" she asked. "From what you've told me about Jessica, she hardly goes on two dates with the same guy."

"Tell me about it. Three dates and you were practically engaged in Jessica's book," Elizabeth said, making a face. She couldn't blame Nina for having trouble believing her. She was still having trouble herself, and she'd had more than a day to get used to it.

Yesterday, after Jessica convinced her to leave her alone, Elizabeth drove two hundred miles along the coast and back again, trying to come to terms with the news and figure out if there was anything she could do to help her twin. By the time she got back to the campus, there was a stack of phone messages from her brother waiting for her and a note from Tom and one from William. But the only person she'd wanted to talk to was Nina. After sitting on the beach by herself for what seemed like hours, she'd decided that there wasn't much she could do for Jessica except be there for her. She could do something for herself, though, and that was share her troubles with her friend.

Nina took a bite of her apple. "Then I guess she and Mike must have had four dates, huh?"

Despite herself, Elizabeth had to smile. "Stop it," she ordered. "This isn't funny. It's bad

30

enough that my parents don't have a clue about what's going on, but as far as I can tell, this isn't exactly a marriage made in heaven."

"Already?" Nina's surprise was rapidly turning into shock. "The honeymoon's over already?"

"It's not only over, they've decided to skip the boring settling-down bit and go straight to domestic violence."

Nina put down her apple and her face turned serious. "You're kidding. He hit her?"

Elizabeth shook her head. "I don't think so, but he hit just about everything else in the apartment."

"And Jessica puts up with that?" Nina demanded. "This is getting worse and worse."

"What am I going to do, Nina?" Elizabeth's eyes filled with tears. For the first time since she walked in on Jessica on Saturday night and found her sobbing in the wreckage of her home, Elizabeth felt her own control slipping. Yesterday, with the ocean sparkling in front of her and a clear blue sky above, she'd managed to convince herself that things weren't as bad as they'd seemed. All couples argued. Especially newly-weds. Especially newlyweds who weren't very good at being part of a couple in the first place. But now that Elizabeth had someone to confide in, she realized how worried she really was.

Nina looked thoughtful. "What about your

31

brother? Have you told him about the marriage? Maybe he could talk to Jess—"

"Forget it." Elizabeth shook her head adamantly. "Steven goes nuts if he hears Mike's name. Billie said it's all she can do to keep him from storming downstairs and beating Mike up. If Steven finds out they're married, he's liable to do something really stupid."

"Oh, Elizabeth. I know how worried you are. If there's anything I can do to help, tell me, okay?" Nina offered. "I don't have much experience as a marriage counselor, but if you want me to go see Jessica with you, I will."

Elizabeth hesitated for a second. Nina and her friend Bryan Nelson had recently been the victims of a racist attack that Elizabeth believed was instigated by the secret society. Because of this, she hadn't been sure if she should tell Nina her suspicions about Mike McAllery or not.

"I know it's a delicate situation," Nina went on, misinterpreting Elizabeth's hesitation. "But you know you can trust me, Elizabeth. I'm your friend."

Elizabeth touched Nina's hand. "I know you're my friend, Nina. You're one of the best friends I've ever had."

The words *but there's something about Mike McAllery I haven't told you yet* were running through Elizabeth's mind, but she couldn't make them come out of her mouth. How could she admit to Nina that she was almost certain her brother-in-law was the man responsible for putting her in the hospital and nearly killing Bryan?

Nina stared back at her, her brown eyes serious. "Is it one of those twin things?" she asked. "You know, you don't like to get other people involved?"

Elizabeth nodded, relieved. There were definitely times when having a twin had its advantages, though Jessica made it easy to forget that. "Got it in one."

Nina laughed. "They don't call me smart for nothing."

"A lot of these young girls today don't seem to realize it, but marriage isn't something you can just take for granted," the woman on the phone-in program was saying. "It's something you have to work at."

Jessica reached over and turned up the volume so that she could hear it over the coffeemaker while she fixed Mike's breakfast. Last night, after Mike fell asleep with his arms around her, she'd lain awake, thinking about being married.

The problem was that as much as she loved Mike, she wasn't used to being married. She didn't know how to do it; she was never sure what to expect. Marriage wasn't like dating, or even like having a serious boyfriend. You lived

33

with one person and you couldn't do anything without thinking how they'd react to it. It had been bad enough when she'd lived at home and had to tell her parents where she was going and what she was doing and when she'd be back, but this was even worse. You couldn't ever just think of yourself; you always had to think of your partner, too. But if you really loved someone, it was worth it, she'd decided, and she really loved Mike. She was going to work at their marriage, just as the woman on the radio said.

"My name's Damion, and I'll tell you what I think's important in a marriage," said a new voice on the radio. "I think it's important to keep the magic alive. You know, a guy doesn't want to come home and find his wife sitting around in her nightgown with all the dishes in the sink. He wants to come home to a real babe."

Magic, thought Jessica as she beat up the eggs. *Real babe. I can do that part with no trouble.*

Elise from Tudanco came on the line. Elise thought that marriage was about compromise. "You can't expect to get things your own way all the time," she said. "It's a matter of give-and-take."

Jessica popped the toast into the toaster. *Give-and-take. I can dig that. That's not too bad.*

Hector was next. "No marriage can work if the people are too similar," he said. "You know what I mean? If you have two people who are

34

loud and noisy or bossy, then they'll drive each other nuts. Or two people who are always running around; then they'll never see each other."

Mike and I should be all right, Jessica assured herself as she started to scramble the eggs. *Our temperaments are completely different.*

"That last guy has it all wrong," Meredith from Santa Ana called in to say. "People who have a lot in common have a much better chance of a successful marriage than people who don't. What's the point of living with someone who likes to get up at five A.M. if you don't like to go to bed till five A.M.?"

Jessica didn't know. What Meredith was saying made sense. But that wasn't a problem either. After all, she and Mike had a lot of things in common. They definitely liked to go to bed at the same time.

Mike came into the kitchen just as Pat from Shady Grove was saying that she thought the most important thing in a marriage was to talk things through and always be honest. "Never go to bed angry," Pat said. "And never start the day with a fight."

"Hey, I just had the greatest idea," Mike said, scooping her up in his arms.

"You're going to ruin the eggs," Jessica scolded him, though she didn't exactly push him away. She turned and kissed him on his chin. "What's your greatest idea?"

35

He grinned. "Now that you've told your family about us, why don't we have your sister and brother over for dinner? I could make my meltdown chili."

Talk things through, Pat had said. *Always be honest.* They'd talked things through, and she had been honest. She'd told him that she'd told Elizabeth they were married; it wasn't her fault that he'd assumed she'd told Steven and her parents, too. It wasn't her fault that he couldn't understand how difficult it was for her to tell them.

Jessica smiled back at him enthusiastically. "Gee," she said, "that sounds terrific. I'll ask them today."

On the radio Mary from Limona was explaining why she and her husband had been happily married for fifty years. Jessica reached up and turned Mary off.

Todd Wilkins was knotting his tie in front of the full-length mirror on the bathroom door. His shirt had just come back from the laundry, his slacks were creased, his shoes shone. He didn't look like a cheat or a criminal. He looked like a young man with a future, not a young man with a shady past. There wasn't a mother in the country who wouldn't look at him and think, *What a nice boy.*

"You look good," he told his reflection, but

he sounded more confident than he felt.

Two slim, tanned arms wrapped themselves around him from behind. "Of course you look good," said the sleepy voice of Lauren Hill. Her tousled copper-colored head appeared next to his in the mirror. "You are good, Todd." She nuzzled his neck, her breath warm against his skin. "You're great."

At any other time, being told he was great by a beautiful woman would have bolstered Todd's confidence no end, but this morning she might as well have told him he had dandruff.

"Let's hope the dean and the ethics committee agree with you," he answered sourly.

Lauren's lips traced a line along his jaw to his ear. "Forget about them," she whispered, pressing against him. "Let me give you a few good-luck kisses."

Why couldn't she understand how nervous he was? Ever since the sports scandal had broken, Lauren had refused to take his fears seriously. Gently, he disengaged her arms from around his chest. "Not now, Lauren. Mark'll be here any minute."

"So what?" Her arms encircled him again. "Mark's seen us kiss before."

He pulled away, this time not so gently. "Lauren, please. I can't deal with this right now. Mark and I are going to be interrogated in thirty minutes. Our whole university careers are on the line."

37

"Oh, stop being so melodramatic." She tossed her hair over her shoulder, a sign that she was annoyed. "You're not being *interrogated*. The committee just wants to ask you a couple of questions." She came around to the front of him, putting her arms around his neck. "You have nothing to worry about, Todd. You didn't do anything wrong."

"I know I didn't do anything wrong, and you know I didn't do anything wrong, but I'm not so sure the university sees it that way. They're acting like I took bribes."

Of course he hadn't done anything wrong. Todd, like the other top athletes, had received some preferential treatment from the first day he set foot on campus, but it hadn't occurred to him that there was anything immoral or illegal in it. That was the way jocks were treated. Superathletes brought money and attention to colleges, and in exchange they were treated like princes; that was the way things worked. At least it had been the way things worked before Elizabeth Wakefield and Tom Watts decided to do an exposé on the SVU sports department on the campus television station.

"Well, we all know who you guys have to thank for that," Lauren said, as though reading his thoughts. She brushed her lips against his. "Maybe you shouldn't have dumped Elizabeth for me," she teased. "Then none of this would have happened."

Todd could see his reflection in her eyes. *And what if I'm found guilty and they throw me off the team?* he wondered. *Who's going to get dumped then?* It was hard to imagine Lauren Hill dating a has-been basketball player with a black mark on his record.

"Maybe I shouldn't have," he answered, kissing her back so she'd know he was kidding.

Alexandra Rollins lay on Mark Gathers's bed, watching him get ready for his meeting with the dean.

If he reknots his tie one more time, I'm going to scream, she thought. Swearing, he yanked the dark-blue silk apart again. Immediately she felt disloyal. She knew he was going through hell, and the investigation hadn't even begun in earnest yet.

"You look fine, Mark," she said out loud. "You've got to try to relax a little."

"Relax? You want me to relax?" His eyes found hers in the mirror. "It's easy for you to talk, Alex—you're not the one going down the tubes."

She stifled a sigh. They had had this argument before. In fact, since it had become obvious that he was one of the SVU players under the most suspicion in the sports scandal, she and Mark had done almost nothing but argue about what would happen to him. The other athletes spent most of their time protesting their innocence, but Mark spent his imagining doom. Worst of all, though, the more supportive Alex tried to be, the more Mark shunted her aside.

"You don't know that that's going to happen," she said, keeping any trace of annoyance out of her voice. "Maybe you'll have this preliminary meeting with the dean and that'll be it. Maybe you'll get off with just a reprimand. Lauren says—"

"Don't tell me what Lauren Hill says." He yanked his tie so hard, she was afraid he might choke himself. "Lauren Hill talks out of her makeup case. She lives in la-la land, where all the girls are cheerleaders and all the guys used to be Boy Scouts. This is the real world, Alex. You don't get a happy ending just because you want one."

"You haven't done anything that everybody else didn't do," she said as she slipped from the bed. "You're being too hard on yourself—"

"I'm not being half as hard on me as the ethics committee is going to be," he said, swinging around to face her.

Alex put her hands on his broad shoulders. "Mark," she said gently, staring into his troubled eyes. "I know what you're going through, but you've got—"

"You don't know what I'm going through, Alex." He pushed her hands away and pulled his jacket from its hanger. The hanger clattered to the floor. "You couldn't."

"I could if you'd confide in me," she protested, following him as he strode across the room. "I'm your girlfriend, Mark. I care about you. I could help you if you'd let me."

"Nobody can help me!" Mark shouted. He put on his jacket, gave himself one last look in the wall mirror, and opened the door. "I'm all on my own."

"No, you're not!" Alex cried as the door slammed behind him. "I'm here."

The tears she'd been holding back since she woke up and found Mark already half-dressed and in a bad mood filled her eyes. "I'm here," she said again in a choked whisper. "Why do you shut me out?"

Elizabeth's drink sat untouched on the table in front of her. Her eyes were on Billie's face, trying to judge her reaction to what she'd just told her. "Well?" Elizabeth prompted. "What do you think? Don't you think it makes sense that Mike could be the leader of the secret society?"

Billie smiled wryly. "I think it's a good thing your brother's not here." She rolled her eyes. "He'd be out that door and after Mike McAllery quicker than you can say 'motorcycle.'"

"Yeah. I know." Elizabeth picked up her spoon and put it down again. "I wasn't even going to tell you at first, except I don't have anyone I can talk to about it. Steven's out of the question, and so is Nina. I tried to tell her, but I just kept seeing her lying in the hospital and I couldn't do it." She picked up the spoon again, turning it over in her hand. "And I miss not being able to talk to Jess."

Billie gave her a sympathetic look. "I'm glad you told me, Elizabeth, I really am. I may not be Jessica, but I do think of you almost as my sister." She took a sip of her tea. "And I promise I won't mention this to Steven. He's nuts enough about Jess and Mike without giving him something else to worry about."

Elizabeth felt a little thrill of anxiety shoot through her. "So you do think I'm right, then?" she asked. "You think Mike is responsible for the attack on Nina and Bryan."

"Slow down, Elizabeth." Billie held up her hand. "I didn't say I thought you were right." She absentmindedly folded her empty sugar wrapper in half, and then in half again. "That's a pretty serious accusation, you know," she went on, carefully choosing her words. "You and your brother don't like Mike McAllery, but being a little wild and being the leader of a secret society aren't necessarily the same thing. I just hope you're not letting your emotions get in the way of your head."

"Of course I'm not," Elizabeth said. "I'm a

reporter, Billie. I'm trained to be objective."

"Um," Billie said, a slight smile on her lips. "But even reporters have feelings. And Jessica is your twin. Are you sure you're not just trying to protect her?"

I wish I could protect her, Elizabeth thought, *but it's a little late for that.* For a second she was tempted to tell Billie about the marriage and Mike's violent temper, but she decided against it. Reporters weren't the only ones with feelings. Billie's might lead her to tell Steven, and then who knew what would happen.

Elizabeth picked up her cold cup of coffee. "I'm sure, Billie, I really am. I've been working on this secret society story for a while now and getting nowhere. But Mike being the leader makes sense. It makes everything fit into place."

"But you don't have any real evidence," Billie argued. "All you know is that he has money he doesn't seem to work too hard for, he's around campus a lot, no one knows very much about him, he's got a reputation as a tough guy, and he has a temper." She broke off a piece of her doughnut and pointed it at Elizabeth. "We could be describing the Lone Ranger, too, you know. None of those things make him a power-crazed thug."

"Well, no . . ." Elizabeth said reluctantly. "When you put it like that, I guess the evidence does seem a little circumstantial." It was amaz-

43

ing how when she went through the points against Mike McAllery in her own mind, they didn't seem circumstantial at all; they seemed completely conclusive.

"A little?" Billie popped the piece of doughnut into her mouth. "It's a little circumstantial like Mount Everest is a little mountain."

"I didn't say I was ready to run the story yet," Elizabeth defended herself. "I still have a lot of research to do, but at least it's something to go on. It's a place to start."

Billie nodded. "You're right," she said. "It's a place to start." She picked up her tea. "I just wonder where it'll end."

Tom glanced at the clock tower at the north end of the quad as he fought his way through the throng of students going to their classes. He'd looked up Elizabeth's schedule in the office, so he knew that she had English in three minutes. He didn't even care if he talked to her anymore; he just wanted to see her and make sure she was all right. She still hadn't returned when he brought Celine back to her room after lunch yesterday, and she wasn't in the cafeteria for breakfast.

Maybe he was overreacting, but since the night he was roughed up by a bunch of secret society thugs on his way back to his dorm, he'd been more worried about Elizabeth's safety than ever. He'd pretended to Danny and Isabella, who had found him, that the guys who jumped him had been after money, but they hadn't been. They'd been giving him one last warning to keep his nose—and Elizabeth's—out of their business.

Where could she be? he asked himself for the thousandth time as he ran through a break in the crowd. *If she's all right, why hasn't she called me?* He answered his own question as he jumped a stone bench. *Because she's mad at you, you jerk. Because she thinks you'd rather work with Celine than with her.*

Tom had been so worried about the anonymous threats that had been made against him and Elizabeth if they continued working on the secret society story that he'd tried to discourage Elizabeth by pretending that Celine was helping him. Even he had to admit it wasn't one of his better ideas. Not only hadn't it worked, it had backfired. He was beginning to think the only way he'd ever get rid of Celine would be to move to Nebraska.

A hand fell on his arm, pulling him to a sudden stop.

"Where are you off to in such a hurry, sugar? You'd think the men with the searchlights and the guns were after you, the way you were tearing along."

Tom groaned inwardly as he turned around.

Think of the devil and there she was, dressed in bright pink and smiling her most dazzling smile.

"Not now, Celine," he said, continuing to move forward. "I'm late to meet someone in the English building."

Celine moved with him, her bright pink nails curled around his arm like the talons of some exotic tropical bird. "I'll come with you," she said breezily. "I'm going that way myself."

He sped up his pace, dragging her with him. It didn't matter if Elizabeth saw him with Celine; all that mattered was that he saw Elizabeth.

"Slow down, lover," Celine squealed, tightening her grip. "I've got three-inch heels on, you know, not cleats."

"Celine," Tom snapped, not slowing down. "I'm in a hurry. If you can't keep up with me, then I'll have to go without you. I don't have time for your three-inch heels."

Celine pouted. "If I didn't know better, I'd think I had bad breath or something," she said. "First the Little Princess avoids me for two days and now you won't even walk me to my class."

He stopped so abruptly that she would have sailed right past him if she hadn't been holding on. Instead she pitched forward, nearly losing her balance.

"Elizabeth is avoiding you? You mean she hasn't come back yet?"

Celine brushed a wayward strand of hair

from her face. "Oh, she came back," she said, "but I haven't seen her. I was out by the time she got back last night and she was gone by the time I got up this morning."

Tom was so relieved to know that Elizabeth was all right that he almost hugged Celine. Almost, but not quite. Getting into a clinch with Celine would be like jumping into quicksand holding a fifty-pound weight: he'd never get out.

"Of course," Celine said, her eyes watching him carefully, "I don't suppose she really is avoiding me." She smiled. "I figure she's just very, very busy with the charming William White."

Tom didn't smile back. Not only did Tom think William White was about as charming as strychnine, the too-sweet tone of Celine's voice made it clear what she thought Elizabeth was very, very busy at. Which wasn't as bad as what he'd been imagining. Even Tom had to admit that an Elizabeth spending her time with William White was better than an Elizabeth kidnapped by the secret society—if only marginally.

"But that's all right, isn't it, sugar?" Celine slipped her arm through his again. "Because I'm very, very busy with you."

Jessica was stretched out in the back of the Buick that Mike was working on, her pretty face buried in a women's magazine. On the floor beside her were several more magazines. When she'd told Mike about being fired from the coffeehouse, he'd actually been happy. "That's great," he'd said with a grin. "That'll give you more time to hang out with me."

So here she was, fulfilling her roll as the perfect wife by hanging out with Mike. At least it was more fun than staying in the apartment doing homework by herself.

"So have you found any good recipes?" he called up to her.

"Not yet," she called back. "They all seem to be disgustingly healthy this month. You know, brown rice and stir-fried vegetables with that bean curd stuff. I don't want everyone to think we can't afford real food."

Mike thought that she'd bought all these magazines so she could plan the dinner she was making for her sister and brother. Jessica wasn't sure how she was going to get out of this dinner, since she had no intention of inviting anyone to it, but until she figured out that one minor detail she was at least enjoying the magazines. They were crammed full of fascinating articles and advice columns on relationships, and they were more gripping than a soap opera. As far as Jessica could tell, there wasn't a couple in the galaxy who didn't have problems. If they didn't have problems with sex, they had problems with money. If they didn't have problems with money, then they couldn't agree on where to go on their vacations. If they agreed on what movies to see and where to spend Christmas, then they couldn't agree on what color to paint the living room or what to name the dog. She might not be learning much about cooking, but she was learning a lot about what being part of a couple meant: squabbling all the time.

Mike's handsome face, smeared with grease, appeared at the side of the car.

"Maybe we should make something you know they like," he suggested, "instead of taking any chances." He winked. "There should be one thing in the house that your brother likes, since he sure as hell doesn't like me."

Jessica closed the magazine on the article about the couple who hated each other's music so much that the wife used her husband's favorite CD to play Frisbee with the dog.

"No," she said, shaking her head. "I want to make something incredibly sophisticated that neither of them has ever had before. Something really special." *And serve it in Wyoming,* she added to herself.

He leaned over and kissed the side of her face. "Speaking of something special," he said. "I don't suppose you'd like to come under the car with me?"

She swatted him with the magazine. "Leave me alone, you animal," she said with a laugh, kissing the one clean spot on his cheek. "Having this dinner was your idea, remember."

"Yeah, I remember," he said with a grin. "And I'm really looking forward to it. Friday should be quite a night."

Jessica grinned back. "Yes," she said. "It certainly should."

Chapter
Three

Elizabeth was glad Nina had invited her to have lunch with her and Bryan. Nina and Bryan had so much good humor and energy that for the first time in days Elizabeth had been able to forget her problems for a while. Bryan even managed to make his stay in the hospital sound funny.

Nina scooped the pickles from her hamburger and passed them to Bryan. "Bryan and I were talking about your investigation of this secret society, Elizabeth," she said, "and we want you to know that you can count on us for any help you need."

Bryan nodded. "We're as determined to find out who's behind this thing as you are," he said to Elizabeth as he passed Nina the slice of tomato from his sandwich. He grinned. "Now that my wounds have healed, I'm ready to start fighting again."

"Yeah," Nina said, giving him a nudge. "He wants to see if he can crack the rest of his ribs."

Elizabeth smiled ruefully. "I'm hoping we can avoid any more violence. After all, the pen *is* mightier than the sword."

"I think you've led a sheltered life," Bryan teased her. "Where I come from, brass knuckles are a whole lot more persuasive than your average sonnet, and you remember them longer."

Elizabeth was about to come back with a flippant reply when out of the corner of her eye she noticed William White sitting at the other side of the cafeteria with Celine. She could feel him watching her. She fixed her eyes on her lunch.

Somehow, the presence of William made her think how lucky Nina was. Being beaten up in a racist attack hadn't been lucky at all, but both she and Bryan had survived it—and survived it together. Nina and Bryan were clearly falling in love, but more than that, they shared the same interests and values. Nina and Bryan were so well suited for each other that it made Elizabeth wonder if she was ever going to find the man who matched her perfectly. She used to think that man was Todd, but time had proved her wrong. There had even been moments when she'd thought that man might be William, but she couldn't seem to get her heart to agree.

Elizabeth took up a forkful of salad. Her

heart was stubbornly backing Tom Watts, despite the fact that Tom Watts was about as interested in Elizabeth as he was in tree surgery.

"It's really weird, isn't it?" Bryan was saying. "You look around at this cafeteria and everything seems perfect. Everybody seems so nice and normal. It's hard to imagine that some of the people sitting here, worrying about their midterms and joking about their professors, are so filled with hatred that they'd actually try to kill someone."

Elizabeth looked up at him, Tom and William instantly forgotten. *You think that's something*, she felt like saying. *It's even harder to imagine that the man who controls all that hatred is married to my sister.*

Celine stabbed at a slice of carrot, wishing it were William White's heart.

He'd invited her to have lunch with him, but once he'd found out that she hadn't discovered where Elizabeth had been the other night or how her investigation for WSVU was coming, he'd lost all interest in her. For the last ten minutes he'd been sitting across from Celine moodily sipping a cup of coffee while she tried to make conversation. She might as well have been a recorded message for all the attention he was paying to her.

"I'm really looking forward to the charity

ball," Celine said, gamely talking on despite the fact that William was looking everywhere but at her. "It's so nice to be able to spend a lot of money on a dress, have a good time, and still feel like you've done something worthwhile."

He raised his cup to his lips, but instead of drinking he held it there, his eyes staring over the rim. Just for a second, Celine thought she saw the shadow of something that might be anger or even jealousy in those ice-blue eyes.

She looked over her shoulder, following his gaze. *I should have known,* she thought furiously as her eyes fell on Elizabeth, Nina, and Bryan. *Princess Purity is the only thing that ever makes William show any emotion.* She turned back to her plate and lashed out at a sliver of cucumber, spraying salad dressing over her companion's immaculate shirt. Not that he noticed, of course. He was too busy studying every movement Elizabeth Wakefield made. *Serves him right,* she thought spitefully. *I hope the stain doesn't come out.*

"What a cozy little threesome they make," she said, her voice sweet again. "It's so nice to see racial harmony at work, isn't it?"

"I didn't realize Bryan was out of the hospital already," William said. "I thought he'd been very badly hurt."

"He was very badly hurt," Celine said, grateful to have him finally talking to her, even if he was still looking at Elizabeth. "But now he's better."

54

"And what about the investigation into the attack?" William asked, his voice as casual as if he were asking about her lunch. "Do you know if Bryan remembered anything that would help the police?"

Celine waggled her fork at him. "I told you, sugar, I haven't really seen Elizabeth since Saturday. She's been busy. And anyway," she went on, "you know as well as I do that she wouldn't say anything to me. The only thing we exchange is insults."

"What about her notes?" he asked. "I thought you were keeping an eye on them."

Celine locked her mouth in a smile. For two cents, she'd dump her bowl of salad over his head. This wasn't the way she had planned things, she keeping an eye on Elizabeth's notes and William keeping an eye on Elizabeth. By now, according to Celine Boudreaux's timetable, William White should be keeping his eyes, and one or two other parts of his body, on her.

"I can't keep an eye on them if she isn't working on them, can I, sweetie? For the fiftieth time, William, Little Miss Perfect hasn't been around for the last couple of days."

"Well, where has she been?" he mumbled, but so softly that she knew he really wasn't speaking to her.

"I think the answer to that question may have just walked in the door," Celine said, her own attention now caught by the tall, dark figure standing in the entrance, searching through the crowd. Celine's spirits rose. Tom was probably looking for her. "I mean, except for you and Nina Harper, Tom Watts is the Princess's only friend, isn't he?" She turned back to William with a killer smile.

She needn't have bothered. William was gone.

Tom felt like a man who had been crawling across the desert on his hands and knees for two days and suddenly sees a lush green oasis up ahead. Elizabeth was safe. She was sitting with Nina and Bryan, laughing and talking, totally oblivious to the fact that he'd been going out of his mind with worry since Saturday night.

For several seconds Tom just stood in the doorway of the cafeteria, watching her. Elizabeth was beautiful, there was no denying that, but it wasn't just her beauty that made his heart ache with longing whenever he was near her.

Elizabeth Wakefield was more than eyes the color of a summer sea and hair like spun gold. She had one of the finest minds he'd ever encountered and a passionate nature. She was so much like him in her spirit and values that it was almost funny that she didn't seem to know it. Instead, she was interested in William White.

Thinking about William made Tom's jaw clench. There was a time, long ago, when Tom and William traveled in the same circles. Tom hadn't liked him even then. There was something too perfect about William; too perfect and too smooth. Plus, Tom didn't like his eyes. William had the kind of eyes Tom always imagined the devil would have, almost hypnotically attractive but empty and hard.

Tom gave himself a shake. "Never mind Mr. White," he mumbled to himself. "You have to talk to Elizabeth. Now." He had to find out what her big discovery was, but more than that he had to tell her the truth about getting beaten up, or the next time she disappeared for a couple of days his heart might not be the only thing that was injured.

Bryan saw him first. "Yo, dude!" Bryan called, raising one hand in greeting. "If it isn't the tireless crusader for truth and justice, our own Thomas Watts."

"I see they've taken the bandages off," Tom replied, grinning back. Bryan had once helped him with a piece on campus discrimination, and ever since they'd been friendly. "I guess that means you'll be getting into trouble again."

"I'm counting the minutes," Bryan said.

Elizabeth turned around at the sound of his voice. He could tell from the way she smiled at him that she'd forgotten about their fight over Celine—or at least decided to forgive him. Tom wondered if he had William White to thank for that or not.

"Tom!" Elizabeth cried. "I've been looking for you."

She'd been looking for him? Where, in her shoes?

"Well, that's funny," he said, wishing he could just hold her in his arms for a second to make sure she was real, "because I've been looking all over for you." He nodded at the empty chair between Bryan and Elizabeth. "Mind if I join you?"

"Of course not," Elizabeth answered immediately. "Sit down."

But before he could move around Elizabeth and take a seat, a long, pale hand took hold of the chair and pulled it out.

"I'm afraid this seat's already taken," William White informed him, smoothly sliding into place.

What is it about this guy's smile that makes me want to put my fist in it? Tom wondered.

Elizabeth looked confused, a faint blush staining her cheeks. "Why don't you pull up another chair, Tom?" She looked around. "There's plenty of room."

William leaned back, an amused expression on his face. "I'm sure Tom doesn't have time for something as ordinary as lunch, Elizabeth," he said. "Tom's too busy righting wrongs and bringing the bad guys to justice, aren't you, Watts?" He grinned at Nina and Bryan. "We all sleep easier knowing Tom's on the job, don't we?"

Part of Tom wanted to stay right there. *You want to fight, Mr. White, then we'll fight,* he felt like saying. But another part of him didn't want to bother. What was the point of staying and trading underhanded insults with William White for the next half hour? What would it prove? Elizabeth would think it was petty jealousy on his part and everyone else would just be bored.

"Thanks for the offer," Tom said, his eyes on Elizabeth. "But William's right; I've got a lot of work to do." He put his hand on the back of Elizabeth's chair and leaned so close to her that his face almost touched hers. "Maybe you could drop by the studio later," he said, too softly for anyone else to overhear. "I really need to talk to you." He saw the angry look flash through William's eyes because he was expecting it.

One point for my team, Tom thought.

"You're sure you don't mind?" Jessica asked. She watched Isabella cross into the bedroom, listening until she heard her shut the bathroom door behind her. Then, her voice too low to be heard by Isabella, she said, "I'll try not to be too long, sweetie, but you don't want a stupid wife, do you? You want me to pass my midterms. Isabella doesn't have much free time to help me."

"Of course I don't mind," Mike said, sounding surprised that she should suggest such a thing. "You take as long as you want, baby. I'll grab something to eat at the diner and do some extra work on the Buick. I've almost cracked the wiring problem."

Jessica smiled to herself. It worked. All she had to do was make him think that she'd told Isabella they were married and he was fine. Now if only she could make him think that he was eating with Steven and Elizabeth on Friday night without actually having them in the apartment, and everything would be better than fine.

"I'll see you later, then," Jessica said quickly as she heard the bathroom door open again. "I won't be too late. I just have a couple of hundred years of wars in Europe to commit to memory."

"Sounds a lot easier than the wiring of the Buick," Mike said. "You be careful, baby. Drive slowly coming home, okay?" He made a kissing sound. "I'll be waiting for you."

"Okay, honey. You be careful, too. Kiss kiss."

"Kiss kiss."

When Jessica hung up the phone and turned around, Isabella was sitting on the sofa, smirking at her. *"Kiss kiss?"* she teased. "Don't tell me you've got Mike McAllery saying kiss kiss back, Jess, because that I won't believe."

"Well, you can believe it," Jessica said, "because he said it. He even makes the noise."

Isabella groaned exaggeratedly. "You'll get him to cut his hair and start wearing a suit next."

There's not much chance of that, Jessica thought. *The only things I can get him to do are the things he wants to do.* Mike obviously hadn't read any of the articles on compromise in marriage that she'd been reading. Not that she was going to admit that to her friend. "You never can tell," she answered smugly.

"I'm not saying I think I was wrong about Mike or anything," Isabella began, giving her a shrewd look. "But I admit that I'm surprised you two have lasted this long and are still acting like the Romeo and Juliet of Sweet Valley U."

Jessica threw herself onto the sofa beside her. "From what you were telling me, I thought you and Danny were the Romeo and Juliet on this campus."

Isabella grinned broadly. "I do think Danny and I could give you and Mike the Mechanic a run for your money." She wrapped her arms around her knees. "I know I said this before, Jess, but he is so *wonderful.* I really never felt like this before about anyone. It's like being in love with your very best friend in the entire world, who just happens to be one of the most gorgeous men you've ever known. It's incredible."

"You're right," Jessica said, managing somehow to keep the smile on her face. It had never

61

struck her before how astoundingly boring a woman in love could be if the woman wasn't you. "You did tell me this before. About thirteen times." How was she ever going to understand the events leading up to World War I if all Isabella wanted to talk about was Danny?

Isabella laughed. "Okay, okay," she said good-naturedly. "We'll get back to Eastern Europe. I can see you're showing a little love-talk fatigue."

"Listen who's talking," Jessica said. "You never let me yak about Mike the way you've been yakking about Danny."

"That's because Danny is an all-around upstanding, nice guy, and Mike McAllery is a cross between Jesse James and Evel Knievel."

Jessica winced. Not that long ago she would have argued with Isabella about the fairness of this description, but by now she had seen the dark side of Mike McAllery enough times to know there was more truth in it than she'd like to admit.

Generous as only a woman in love can be, Isabella put an arm around Jessica's shoulders. "I'm just teasing, you know," she said. "To tell you the truth, feeling like this about Danny has made me think about you and Mike a little more. I mean, I know he's never been my type, but if you love him that much and he loves you, well, who am I to criticize?"

"Really?" Jessica asked, wishing that Isabella

had felt this generous a few weeks ago, before Jessica's own feelings became so confused.

"Yeah, really." Isabella gave her a hug. "After all, love changes people, doesn't it? Maybe finding you was what Mike needed to straighten himself out."

Jessica smiled back, but she couldn't quite make herself speak. *Marriage changes people more,* she was thinking. *And not always for the better.*

Elizabeth twirled her spaghetti around her fork absentmindedly, only half-listening to what William was saying.

"Elizabeth!" He snapped his fingers in front of her face. "You're not still mad at me for what happened at lunch, are you?"

She shook her head. "No, I'm not still mad." She gestured to the elegant room. Its white-washed walls were lit by pewter lanterns, and handmade wrought-iron tables, each one with a different-colored glass top, covered its polished wood floor. To apologize for being so rude to Tom, William had met her outside her last class with a white rose and an invitation to dinner. "How could I be mad when you take me to such great restaurants?"

"Then what's wrong?" he asked. "The way you're acting, you'd think you were eating dry shredded wheat instead of the best pasta with red pesto sauce this side of the Atlantic. Are you worried about midterms?"

Elizabeth laughed. Since she'd spent the beginning of the semester with nothing to do but study, she was probably one of the few people on campus who wasn't worried about midterms. "No, I'm not worried about that."

He made a face, as though concentrating hard. "Is it the Queen of Darkness? Has our dear Celine been annoying you again?"

"Celine always annoys me."

He took her hand across the table. His touch was as gentle as a feather's. "Then what is it, Elizabeth? You've been preoccupied all evening."

Elizabeth looked into William's cool blue eyes. Sometimes there was something distant about him that made her feel vaguely uneasy, and sometimes he was so warm and caring that he made her wonder why she ever felt uneasy around him.

He poured some more wine into her glass. "Come on," he urged. "Take another sip of the Chardonnay and tell me what's troubling you. You know I hate to see you like this."

"It's Jess," Elizabeth admitted at last. "Well, not Jess herself, but Mike. Mike McAllery."

At the mention of Mike's name the encouraging smile that had been on William's lips vanished completely. Steven Wakefield wasn't the only one who thought Mike McAllery was the

64

worst thing since the bubonic plague.

"Mike McAllery?" William repeated. "What has he got to do with *you*?"

Elizabeth wasn't going to say anything to William about her new suspicions, because William had never been convinced that the secret society even existed. But before she could stop herself, she was telling him her new theory.

"Don't you see," she said after she'd explained her reasoning. "It all fits. In fact, it fits so perfectly I can't figure out why it took me so long to see it. No one would ever suspect Mike because he isn't really involved in campus life. And no one would ever connect him with Peter Wilbourne and the Sigmas either, that's for sure. It's the perfect cover." A little worried that William might react the way Billie had, Elizabeth rushed on. "And he's got the right personality: egocentric, arrogant, always wanting everything his way . . ."

It took a second for Elizabeth to realize that rather than looking skeptical, William was nodding in agreement. "You know, I think you may have something here," he said when she finally gave him a chance to speak. "It does make sense."

"You think so?" Elizabeth couldn't hide her excitement. Though her feelings for William often weren't clear even to her, she did respect his intelligence and judgment. "You really think so?"

William nodded again. "Absolutely. Peter

Wilbourne's got the right sort of prestige and connections, and Mike's got the street smarts and the will." He picked up a breadstick and broke it in half. "There's only one thing that bothers me."

Elizabeth sighed. There was always "one thing" that bothered someone. "It's Mike and Peter Wilbourne working together, isn't it?" she asked. "They're such an unlikely partnership."

"But as you said, that's actually to their advantage." He shrugged. "No, the thing that bothers me is that neither of them really has the brains to be running something like this."

Elizabeth took another sip of her wine. "I know Peter's about as sharp as an eraser," she said, "but Mike isn't stupid. From what I can gather, he's a pretty clever guy."

"Clever, yes," William agreed. "But clever isn't enough in this case, if you ask me. Whoever's behind this society of yours has to be more than clever. He has to have real foresight and management skills. He has to have the sort of mind that sees problems before they exist."

Elizabeth gazed into her glass, thinking. William had a point. The secret society wasn't a street gang, it was a sophisticated and complex organization, probably with national connections. Unless Mike McAllery was one of the greatest actors of the twentieth century, it didn't seem likely that he was running it. She looked up. "I see what you mean," she admitted. "But I still think Mike's involved. He just has to be."

"Oh, I think Mike's involved, too," said William. "I'm not suggesting that he isn't."

Elizabeth's sea-green eyes darkened in puzzlement. "But—"

"All I'm saying is that there may be someone else working with Mike. Peter's obviously just a pawn in this game, and Mike's the power, but there could be someone else, way in the distance, calling the shots. Someone who has the right background and contacts, and the right sort of mind."

Elizabeth shook her head. She had the feeling that William wasn't just talking abstractly, that he actually had someone in mind, but she couldn't imagine who it could be. "I don't understand. Who?"

William stared at her as though he were willing her to see what he saw. He picked up his wine. "How should I know?" he asked, bringing the glass to his lips. "I'm just a poet. You're the investigative reporter."

By the time Elizabeth got to WSVU, the station was shut tight. It wasn't unusual for Tom to stay long after everyone else left— sometimes working all night if he had to—but he wasn't there tonight.

"I guess he thought I wasn't coming," Elizabeth told herself as she left the building. "He must have gone back to his room."

As she cut across the campus to Tom's dorm Elizabeth started thinking about her conversation with William again. The more she thought about what he'd said about Mike McAllery, the more sense it made. Mike didn't have the sly, political brilliance of a Machiavelli, he had the savvy brutality of a Genghis Khan.

"But if Machiavelli and Genghis Khan joined forces," Elizabeth muttered as she strode along, "they'd be hard to stop." She pushed open the door of Reed Hall. "The only question now is, Who is Machiavelli?"

Elizabeth stopped in front of room 10. "Tom," she called, knocking gently. "Tom, it's me, Elizabeth. Are you there?"

The door opened almost immediately. Only it wasn't Tom Watts who opened it, it was Isabella Ricci, looking very much at home in someone's old football jersey with no shoes on her feet.

First Celine and now Isabella? For a man who had a reputation of not being very interested in women, Tom Watts wasn't doing too badly.

Elizabeth didn't even try to hide her surprise. "What are you doing here?" she blurted.

Isabella laughed, looking pretty surprised herself. "I'm waiting for Danny."

"Danny?" Elizabeth blushed in confusion.

"Yeah, Danny. He went to get some emergency supplies of peanut-butter ice cream so I can help him study for his Spanish midterm." Isabella grinned. "I take it you're looking for Tom."

Elizabeth nodded. "I tried the TV station, but he wasn't there."

"He isn't here either," Isabella said, gesturing behind her. "But you're welcome to come in and wait if you want. I'm sure he'll turn up eventually."

"Well . . ." Elizabeth hesitated. She didn't want to interrupt Isabella and Danny, but on the other hand, Tom had given her the impression that he really wanted to talk to her.

Isabella gave her a tug. "Oh, come on, Elizabeth, don't get all shy. You can at least leave him a message."

Elizabeth could feel Isabella watching her carefully while she sat at Tom's desk writing a note apologizing for missing him at the studio and asking him to give her a call, as though Isabella were getting up the nerve to say something.

Isabella cleared her throat. "You and Tom are pretty good friends, aren't you?" she asked Elizabeth at last.

Elizabeth looked up. "I don't know about that," she said truthfully. "We've worked closely together, but Tom isn't an easy person to get to know."

69

Isabella drew her eyebrows together. "No," she said musingly, "no, I didn't think he was. He seems to be a guy with a lot of secrets."

"Secrets?" Elizabeth put down the pen. What did Isabella mean by that? Tom was a man of mystery; there was no doubt about that. Every time Elizabeth thought she was close to him, he pulled away again. But there was something in the way Isabella said "secrets" that made Tom sound more sinister than mysterious. "What kind of secrets?"

Isabella leaned her arms on Danny's desk and rested her chin on them. "I don't really know," she said slowly. "I just have this feeling about Tom, that he's hiding something. The other day I saw him with Celine and he seemed so different. Danny said something about that being the old Tom—Wildman Watts, he called him—but he wouldn't say more than that." Isabella sighed. "I'm not trying to stir up trouble, Elizabeth. I like Tom." A faint tinge of pink appeared on her cheeks. "I've always liked him. A lot, if you want the truth. I guess seeing him with the South's Revenge kind of jolted me. I mean, even just the fact that Tom would hang out with someone like that . . . Does it make sense to you?"

Elizabeth stared at the photograph on Tom's desk. Other guys had pictures of their families or their girlfriends on their desks, but not Tom. Tom had a picture of Woodward and Bernstein, the reporters who broke the Watergate scandal.

Tom hanging out with Celine made sense when Tom explained it—he wanted her help on the secret society story because she was so close to Peter Wilbourne. But Isabella was right: it made no sense when you looked at it objectively. Celine stood for everything that Tom despised.

"Danny said it must have something to do with the story Tom's working on. That Tom's going through one of his intense, moody phases," Isabella went on.

It's hard to tell when Tom's going through one of his intense, moody phases and when he isn't, Elizabeth commented to herself.

"I even suggested to Danny that Celine was blackmailing Tom," Isabella said. Seeing the look on Elizabeth's face, she giggled. "All right, all right. I was kidding, Elizabeth, but Danny got so defensive about Tom that it made me wonder. Maybe she isn't blackmailing him, but *something's* going on. He isn't going out with that witch because he thinks she's the girl of his dreams."

A tiny smile came over Elizabeth's face. "Maybe she put a curse on him."

Steven pulled the car over to the curb, looking around at the unfamiliar buildings. "It's Jessica's fault," he muttered as he looked for a

71

street sign. "She's driving me so crazy, I don't even know where I'm going anymore."

He got out of the car and walked to the end of the dingy block, but though the rusted pole that had once held the street sign was still there, the sign itself was gone. Steven sighed. He knew where he was going. He just had no idea where he was.

After he'd picked up the camera Billie had gotten repaired, he'd started thinking about Mike McAllery again, and the next thing he knew he was driving through a section of town he'd never been in before.

"And never want to be in again," he told himself as he turned the corner.

Dark, narrow streets were lined with run-down warehouses and dubious shops. It was the kind of place where the hero in the thriller movie always comes face-to-face with the eight-foot killer with an automatic rifle in his hand.

By the time he'd gone two blocks, Steven was almost wishing the guy with the rifle would show up. Maybe he could get directions from him. There didn't seem to be anyone else around to tell him how to get out of here.

Steven was just about to turn around and head back to the car when he saw a tall, dark figure emerge from a building at the other end of the road. He started to call out when he realized that he recognized the man. It was Mike

McAllery himself. Steven stepped back against the buildings, in case Mike suddenly turned around, but he needn't have worried. Mike crossed the street and disappeared around the next corner.

I should have known this would be the kind of place where he'd hang out, Steven told himself. *He's probably going to some sleazy dive to get drunk or meet a woman.*

It wasn't like thinking. Steven had no memory of having the idea or of making the decision. One second he was standing on the empty street, watching the space where Mike had just been, and the next he was hurrying after him.

Steven turned the corner. Mike was in the middle of the block, whistling as he walked down the street. The way he strolled along, Steven thought, you'd think he was on a beautiful tree-lined boulevard and not in a grimy slum. There were several open garages and workshops on the street, and at almost every one Mike said hi to somebody or stopped to exchange a few words.

Get going, Steven urged Mike silently. He slowed down himself, but he could only walk so slowly and still move. *You don't have to talk to everyone you see.* It was like following the devil through hell and having to wait while he discussed the weather with all the lesser devils.

Steven didn't like the way the men they

passed looked at him. It seemed to him that they were sizing him up. Maybe they thought he was a tourist who'd gotten lost. He'd be lucky if the car was still there when he got back. Steven smiled weakly at a large, grease-covered man who had what looked like a dragon tattooed on his forehead. He'd be lucky if he got back at all.

Mike started walking again, and Steven picked up his pace. Now maybe they would get somewhere. Steven started picturing the kind of bar Mike hung out in. It would be dark and filled with smoke, sleazy women, and guys selling hot watches and video equipment.

Just let me catch him with another woman, Steven begged silently. He could picture it so clearly. He'd walk into the bar and there would be Mike and a woman in a tight dress and fishnet stockings, making out on the pool table. *Please. It isn't much to ask. Then I can end this nightmare once and for all.*

Steven was so engrossed in the image in his mind that he didn't notice that Mike had stopped again and was leaning against a lime-green Thunderbird, talking to the head that was peering out from under it.

There was nothing Steven could do but make a run for it. Just turn around and run back the way he'd come. He was about to do that when Mike looked in his direction. Instead of the usual hostile glare, he actually smiled.

"Steven!" Mike shouted. He seemed surprised, but not as surprised as he should have been. "What are you doing here?"

Steven stared back at him blankly. Usually when he saw Mike he just started shouting, but he wasn't about to do that now. He was outnumbered.

Mike's smile grew. "Don't tell me you came all the way down here just to say you can make it on Friday."

"Make it Friday? Make what?"

"Dinner," Mike said, sounding as though it was the most natural thing in the world, as though they always ate dinner together on Friday night. "You are coming, right?"

Fury won out over fear. "I wouldn't come even if I'd been asked," Steven said.

Chapter
Four

Careful not to disturb Mike, Jessica slipped out of bed before the alarm went off and tiptoed into the bathroom.

If anyone had told Jessica what marriage was really like when she was a little girl, she would have burned her Barbie doll's wedding dress and bought her a set of combat fatigues instead. She gazed at herself in the mirror. Her skin was blotchy and her eyes still looked puffy from crying herself to sleep last night.

"Again," Jessica told her reflection. "Crying myself asleep again."

How naive she'd been, believing the fairy tales about the prince and princess living happily ever after. She'd always imagined that the prince and the princess skipped off to their castle and spent the rest of their lives kissing and calling each other darling, but now she knew the truth.

The prince and the princess skipped off to their castle and spent the rest of their lives yelling at each other and slamming doors.

Jessica rubbed a honey scrub into her face, hoping to counteract the ravages of last night's argument. She'd come back from studying with Isabella only to find Mike sitting in the living room, glaring at some show on the television with the sound turned all the way down. When she asked him what was wrong, he threw the remote at the bookcase.

It wasn't the worst fight they'd had. It was bad, but it wasn't the worst. Because Steven hadn't stayed around long enough to really talk to Mike, Jessica had finally managed to convince him that the reason she hadn't asked Steven to dinner wasn't that she hadn't told him about their marriage yet, but that he was so hostile and unforgiving that she just couldn't face it.

Jessica rinsed her face and applied some cream.

Only now, of course, she was going to have to ask somebody to dinner, and pretty quickly. Somebody like Elizabeth.

The bathroom door opened behind her and Mike's head appeared over her shoulder in the glass. How was it possible for someone to have a temper like that and look like such an angel?

"There you are, baby," he said, his voice still thick with sleep. "I was afraid you'd left me when I woke up and you were gone."

I'm too exhausted to leave you, Jessica thought.

She turned around. "I just wish we could stop arguing all the time," she said. "I love you so much . . ."

He opened his arms and she stepped into them. "I love you, too, Jess, you know that. It's just that when Steven said he hadn't been invited, I figured you still hadn't told him that we were married, that's all. I'm sorry I jumped to the wrong conclusion. I really am."

"What do you want me to do?" she asked, squeezing him hard. "Hire a plane and have it write *Jessica and Mike Are Married* in the sky?"

His hands slowly ran down her back. "That's the best idea you've come up with yet," he said.

An old nursery rhyme was running through Elizabeth's head as she pushed her tray along the breakfast line. *Tom, Tom, the baker's son . . .*

Elizabeth helped herself to an apple and a container of yogurt. Ever since her conversation with Isabella, Tom Watts had been on her mind. She kept hearing Isabella say, "He seemed so different," and imagining Tom striding along with Celine on his arm. Isabella was right: Tom wasn't mysterious, he was secretive. There were more sides and corners to him than anyone she had ever known before.

Tom, Tom, the baker's son . . . Was Tom a baker's son? Or was he the son of a doctor, or a lawyer, or a used-car salesman? She had no idea. He never spoke about his parents, not even in the casual way that people did: *My father's got a car like that . . . My mother can't stand cheese either . . . One time when I went to Mexico with my folks . . .*

For all she knew, he could be a visitor from another planet with no past whatsoever. Did he have brothers or sisters? Had he ever had a dog? Where had he grown up? What school had he gone to? Did his mother send him care packages of homemade cookies? Did he ever write to his parents or call them on the phone?

Elizabeth placed a bran muffin and a carton of juice on her tray. The real question was: What had happened to Wildman Watts?

It doesn't add up, Elizabeth argued with herself, grabbing her tray and heading for the cashier. *What made him change from the biggest athlete the school has ever seen to a dedicated investigative reporter?*

Tom must have had everything any man could want when he was a football star. Money, admirers, girls, constant applause and attention, a future as wide open as the sky over the Pacific. What had made him give it all up?

Nina and Bryan were sitting at a window table, laughing together. Still thinking about

Tom, Elizabeth started toward them. Maybe the next time she was in the library, she should look up Tom Wildman Watts in the back issues of the campus paper. Maybe she could at least discover whether he was the son of a baker or not. It was such a great idea that she couldn't understand why she hadn't thought of it before.

Nina and Bryan looked up as she put down her tray.

"We were just talking about you," Nina said.

"Something good, I hope," Elizabeth said.

"But of course!" Nina's braids swung as she laughed. "We were wondering if you're going to the big charity ball next weekend. We thought maybe we could double-date."

Elizabeth glanced at her watch. She had almost an hour before her next class. Suddenly healthy breakfasts and balls for a good cause seemed incredibly unimportant. What seemed important was finding out what Wildman Watts had been like.

"Look," she said to Nina. "I just remembered something I've got to do. Could you bring this stuff back for me? I'm really sorry, but this is urgent."

Bryan winked. "That sounds like the girl reporter talking," he said, looking at Nina. "What do you want to bet she runs into the first telephone box and changes into a leotard and a red cape?"

*　　*　　*

Yesterday, after his and Mark's interview with the dean, both of them had been too stunned and numb to really discuss it. Todd had gone off to shoot some baskets by himself before he actually faced his classes, and Mark had locked himself in his room for the rest of the day. But today, having recovered from his shock, Todd was in a fighting mood.

"I just can't get over it," he fumed. "The dean wouldn't even listen to us. He already had his mind made up."

"And you're surprised?" Mark passed Todd his coffee and slid into the seat across from him. "I've been trying to tell you this all along, Wilkins. Forget about the Bill of Rights. The dean and his ethics committee not only have their minds made up, they've got us tried and found guilty."

"But why?" Todd opened his sugar packet so roughly that half of it fell onto the table. "We haven't done anything. It wasn't like we were the ones breaking all the rules. We just took what they offered us like anybody would."

Mark raised one eyebrow. "It has to be somebody's fault, doesn't it? Who do you think the dean would rather see take the blame for the way we jocks were treated? You and me, or him and his administration?"

Todd brushed the spilled sugar onto the

82

floor. "You don't think this investigation is really going to come up with the truth, do you? You think we're going to take the fall."

Mark gave him a quizzical look over the rim of his cup. "Todd, my man, I think we've already been pushed off the cliff. It's just going to take a little while before we hit the ground." His smile was acidic. "The good news is we'll probably already be dead by the time we do."

Todd pushed his coffee away, his mouth suddenly dry. As worried as he'd been before the meeting with the dean, Todd was so sure in his own heart that he hadn't done anything willfully wrong that he couldn't understand how the dean refused to believe him. The college had offered things to him; he hadn't offered things to the college. It might sound pretty naive now, but he'd simply assumed that was the way things worked.

"I can't believe my life is turning out like this," Todd mumbled, more to himself than to Mark. He'd felt like a prince when he first arrived at SVU. Everyone had made such a fuss over him that he couldn't walk into a room without somebody telling him how great he was. He could still hear the cheering crowds in his head; still see all those pretty girls smiling just at him. It had been like being in heaven. Only now, of course, it was like being in hell. "I had everything going for me when I first got here, and now I'll be lucky if they let me stay."

Mark drank down his coffee. "Personally, I'm beginning to wonder if I even want to stay."

Elizabeth stared into the microfiche, transfixed. If a circus troupe had come banging and tumbling into the library right then, she wouldn't have looked up, not even for a second. War could break out in the reference section and she wouldn't have paid the slightest attention. How could she, when she was looking at Wildman Watts?

It was incredible. Simply incredible. The old Tom Watts, the one who had dominated the sports pages not only of the campus and the local papers but of most of the state papers as well, even looked different from the new Tom Watts. The Tom Watts who Elizabeth knew was darkly handsome but in a remote, quiet way. His was the face you caught at the edge of a crowd and thought, *Now who's that?* There was nothing ostentatious or aggressive about him. In fact, you had to look two or three times before you realized just how attractive he really was.

Wildman Watts had been nothing like that. From what Elizabeth could tell from the newspaper photographs, Wildman Watts had looked and carried himself like a movie star. The face that grinned back at her through the magnifying lens knew that it was good looking and clearly wasn't shy about letting other people know it, too. Cocky and confident, Wildman looked like a young prince who assumed everything he wants is his for the taking—and who is only too happy to take it.

Elizabeth's eyes skimmed the article below the photograph. It made Tom sound like a hero. She slowed down when the piece turned into a mini-interview. When asked what his greatest passion was, Wildman Watts immediately answered, "Football." When asked what he planned to do after college, Wildman didn't hesitate to say, "Play football." When asked what he thought of his fame, he didn't think twice before saying, "I like it."

What about the larger issues in the world? the reporter had wanted to know. Was Tom concerned about pollution, or the destruction of the Amazon, or the famine and violence that dogged the Third World? Apparently not.

Elizabeth's eyes went back to that smugly handsome face. Even though it was obviously the same eyes, the same nose, and the same mouth, she couldn't believe it was the same man. The Tom she knew—or, to be more accurate, the Tom she tried to know—didn't care about fame or success, or very much about football. The Tom who Elizabeth knew was powerfully attracted to issues and principles. She knew people joked about his being a crusader, but a crusader was what he was. He wasn't self-centered: he really cared about the world and wanted to make it better.

"I thought I might find you in here."

Elizabeth caught her breath, automatically turning off the machine before she even looked up into William White's smiling face.

"Researching your piece this early in the morning?" he asked.

Elizabeth smiled. She wasn't sure why, but she didn't want William to know that what she had actually been researching was Tom Watts. "You know what they say," she said, getting ready to leave. "The early reporter gets the scoop."

He handed her a single white rose. "Do they also say that the early guy gets the date to the charity ball?" he asked.

Jessica went through all the favors she had done her sister in the last eighteen years as she parked her brilliant red Karmann Ghia. She couldn't remember that many in detail, but she knew that there must have been thousands, maybe even millions. How many times had she done Elizabeth's chores for her? How many times had she gotten her out of a jam? How many times had she covered for her with their parents?

"She owes me," Jessica told herself as she strode toward the English building. "She definitely owes me."

Not that Jessica was asking Elizabeth for some enormous, out-of-this-world kind of favor. She was asking for nothing, really. In fact, she was doing Elizabeth a favor, inviting her into her home and offering her a delicious meal and an evening of good company. Other sisters would be begging to be invited for dinner. Other sisters would be only too happy to come along, say a few tactful remarks about how their parents couldn't wait to meet their new son-in-law, and kiss everyone good-bye.

At the bottom of the stairs Jessica stopped. Elizabeth was just coming out the door, talking to some dorky guy who looked as if he probably read Shakespeare for fun.

"Elizabeth!" She waved her arms in the air. "Elizabeth!"

Elizabeth didn't always look glad to see her, but she looked glad now. She said something to the guy and came rushing down the steps. This was a good sign. If Elizabeth was that pleased, maybe she'd be easier to convince.

"Jess!" Elizabeth flung her arms around her as though they hadn't seen each other in at least twenty years. "What are you doing here?"

Jessica slipped her arm through her twin's. "I've come to take my favorite sister to the coffeehouse for a cappuccino. You have a free hour, don't you?"

Elizabeth's expression became worried.

"What's wrong?" she asked, her voice slightly hushed. "Has something happened?"

"Of course not." Jessica made a face. "What makes you think something's wrong? I just wanted to see you, that's all. Is that so unusual?"

The worried look was replaced by one that could only be described as wary. It was a look Jessica remembered from high school. Whenever she asked Elizabeth for the teeniest, tiniest favor, Elizabeth got that wary look in her eyes.

Elizabeth stopped short. "What do you want?"

Jessica turned to her in surprised innocence. "Want? What makes you think I want something?"

"Call it a wild hunch," said Elizabeth. She pressed her books close to her chest. "What is it?"

"Come on," Jessica urged, tugging her sister forward. "Let's get some coffee. And maybe some banana cake. Wouldn't you like a nice piece of banana cake?"

Elizabeth wouldn't budge. "I'm not going anywhere until you tell me what you want."

Jessica sighed with exasperation. Of all the twin sisters in the world, why had she gotten the stubbornest one?

She tossed her hair over her shoulder. "It's nothing, Elizabeth, really. In fact, it doesn't even count as a favor. To be honest, Elizabeth,

88

I'm the one who's doing you the favor."

Elizabeth made her mouth go really small. "Oh?"

"Uh-huh." Jessica nodded. "You're going to enjoy it, Elizabeth, I promise."

"Correct me if I'm wrong, Jess," Elizabeth answered, "but haven't I heard that before?"

Jessica shrugged. "Probably. And probably you had a great time."

The blue-green eyes, exactly like Jessica's own, narrowed perceptibly. "What kind of great time are we talking about?"

"Dinner. A fantastic, sophisticated, home-cooked dinner." She started walking away.

Elizabeth followed. "And in whose home is this dinner going to be?" she called after her.

"In mine!" Jessica shouted back.

Elizabeth's hand grabbed hold of her shoulder. "Not so fast, Jess. Are you saying you're inviting me to dinner with you and Mike?" She sounded slightly stunned.

"We do eat, you know," Jessica snapped. Afraid of antagonizing her sister, she added more sweetly, "It'll be fun, Elizabeth, really. You can even bring a date."

Winston sat on the floor of the lounge of Oakley Hall, collapsed in front of a late-afternoon talk show. The couples on television were discussing their marriages with the host, but Winston's mind was filled with snatches of songs. "I'll love you forever . . ." he crooned half under his breath. "Always be mine . . . nothing will change this . . . just give me one night . . . till the seas run dry . . ."

On TV, one of the husbands was showing photographs of his wife's walk-in closet, crammed full of clothes, but Winston didn't see it. Instead he saw the highest, steepest mountain in the world. At its top was a dark-gray castle, covered with vines. Denise Waters came onto the wooden porch of the castle, the screen door banging behind her. Her eyes were on the winding road that led to her door. A convertible Cadillac was racing toward her, its radio blaring and engine roaring. The Cadillac was baby-girl pink and Winston was at the wheel. The car screeched to a halt in front of the castle. "Get in, baby!" Winston shouted. "We're getting out of here! We're going anywhere!"

Winston sighed at the thought of Denise jumping into the passenger seat, ready to go anywhere with him.

On the screen, the husband whose wife had a closet as big as a bedroom was shouting about the number of shoes she had. Winston tried to pay attention. The man's wife had two hundred pairs of shoes. "Two hundred pairs of shoes," Winston told the empty room. He shook his head. Denise would never buy two hundred pairs of shoes. Denise would never give his dog away as one of the wives on the show had done, either. She wouldn't put his cold dinner in his socks because he got home late. She wouldn't go off to Hawaii for a month and leave him all alone. Life with Denise would be perfect.

Once more, Winston gave a lovesick sigh. If only he knew whether she liked him or not.

"She does like you," he corrected himself. "She likes you a lot." They ate together. They studied together. They laughed and joked together. They went to the movies and played pool together. She helped him wash his car and he lent her his best CDs.

But did she like him the way he wanted her to like him—the way he liked her?

"I don't know," Winston admitted. "How can you tell?"

It was a good question. Winston and Denise got along as well as any couple he knew, but he couldn't be sure what her feelings were. When she hugged him, she hugged him like a sister. When she kissed him, she kissed him like a friend. She was always glad to see him, but did that mean that she always *wanted* to see him? After all, Denise Waters was one of the most beautiful, intelligent, and sought-after girls on the SVU campus. Why should she fall in love with goofy Winston Egbert when she could have any BMOC she wanted? On the other hand, though, why shouldn't she?

"What I need is a daisy," Winston decided.

"A daisy?" Denise's clear, lovely laugh tinkled through the room. Winston looked over as she plopped herself down beside him. "What do you want a daisy for, Winnie?"

As usual when suddenly confronted with her presence, Winston couldn't think of anything to say. He couldn't exactly tell her he wanted to ask the daisy if she loved him or not.

"Daisy?" he repeated, feeling himself drowning in her smile. "Did I say daisy?"

Denise nodded. "That's what you said. I heard you clearly. You said you needed a daisy."

Winston could feel himself turning several shades of red. "I didn't say I needed a daisy," he protested feebly, wondering frantically what he was going to tell her he had said. There weren't very many words that rhymed with daisy.

Denise continued to smile back at him expectantly.

One of the wives on the talk show started telling the nation how lazy her husband was. Winston could have flung himself at the television screen and kissed her. "Lazy!" he blurted out. "I said 'I'm feeling lazy.'"

She gave him a quizzical look, but she didn't comment. Instead she turned her attention to the TV. "What's this?" she wanted to know.

"Are they talking about anything interesting?"

"Yes," Winston said quickly. Maybe if she watched a program about couples with him, he could bring up the subject more specifically. *Speaking of couples, Denise,* he could say, *do you have any interest in starting one up?* "Yes, it's very interesting. It's all about married life."

Denise made the face of a beautiful young woman who has just stepped in something unpleasant in open-toed shoes. "Yuck," she said. "I'm going to go back to studying for my French midterm. If there's one thing I can't stand, it's listening to people talk about their marital problems. It's so depressing. It makes you wonder why anyone ever bothers getting married."

It had never made Winston wonder why people got married. People got married because they couldn't live without each other. He watched her get to her feet. "It does?" he managed to ask.

She nodded. "Of course it does, Winnie. I mean, who wants to spend their life arguing about who squeezed the toothpaste in the middle of the tube?"

He'd never really thought of marriage like that. When he thought of spending his life with Denise, toothpaste was never involved. "But marriage isn't about toothpaste," Winston argued as she floated across the room. "Marriage is about love."

Denise turned at the door. "That's what you think," she said.

Tom came out of WSVU into a chill, piercing rain.

"This is just what I need," he muttered as he turned up his collar and started walking toward his dorm. "The perfect end to a perfect day." The only thing that could possibly make things worse would be to bump into Celine before he could reach the safety of his own room. Not that he really had to worry about that too much tonight. Girls like Celine only came out in the rain if they were in a car, preferably an expensive one.

Still edgy from the beating he'd taken, Tom glanced over his shoulder every few seconds as he walked along. He'd been expecting another attack—if not on him, then on Elizabeth—but to his surprise, everything was quiet on the secret society front. There'd been no more dark figures jumping out of the bushes and no more threatening notes.

"It doesn't make any sense," Tom told himself as he crossed the quad. "Why have they gone silent all of a sudden? They must know Elizabeth is still sniffing around." And they probably knew that he was, too.

At the thought of Elizabeth, the depression that had been creeping up on Tom all day started breathing down his neck. He still hadn't had a chance to talk to her. His hanging out with Celine hadn't discouraged Elizabeth from finding out who the leader of the secret society was, but it had certainly discouraged her from having anything to do with him. It seemed as if the only time he saw Elizabeth anymore was when she was with William White.

"William the Ice Man White," Tom grumbled. The depression landed heavily on his shoulders.

Tom had never liked William. Even in the days when they went to the same parties and social functions, Tom hadn't liked him. Tom had been self-centered and arrogant then, he wasn't afraid of admitting that to himself, but he had never been as arrogant and self-centered as William White. It was more than that, though. Tom had never trusted William. He was too smooth, too perfect. You never saw behind that immaculate facade and that smile that gave nothing away.

He and William used to exchange a few polite words from time to time, but Tom had always known that he and William had nothing to say to each other. And then there had been that scene in the fancy restaurant freshman year.

It was after a big game, and the football team and a chosen few friends and followers had gone out to celebrate. Tom, hero of the day, had had a little too much champagne and a little too much admiration to be aware of what was going

95

on, but something had happened with one of the waiters. Either he'd accidentally spilled something on William, or he'd mixed up an order, or he'd talked back when William complained about something. The next thing Tom knew, one of the fraternity brothers was whispering in his ear, "Come outside, Watts, you don't want to miss this. We're going to put that little Mexican guy in his place. It's going to be funny."

But it hadn't been funny. Out in the parking lot, the waiter was surrounded and Peter Wilbourne was pushing him around. The poor guy was terrified, trying to explain half in English and half in Spanish that he hadn't meant to upset anyone, that he hadn't done anything wrong.

Drunk as he was, Tom had known instantly that this wasn't Peter's idea, it was William's. William was standing to one side, watching with his usual coolness, but he was the one running the show.

Mike McAllery knew it, too. He'd been driving by the restaurant that night and had gotten out of his Corvette when he saw what was going on. Mike didn't even look at Peter. He came up to William and put one hand on his arm. Tom never found out what Mike said to William, but he saw William shake Mike off as though he were a bum begging for money. And then Tom—and everyone else—saw Mike McAllery send William White sprawling on the ground. Mike helped the waiter up and walked him back inside the restaurant, not even looking over his shoulder once to see if any of the others were following. None of them were.

The rain got heavier as the dorm came into view.

"How can Elizabeth be fooled by him?" Tom wondered as he loped across the road. "Why doesn't she see that it's all an act? He may talk like a poet, but he's got the heart of a devil." Not that he could come out and say such a thing to Elizabeth, of course. If he told her about that night, she'd think he was making it up because he was jealous of William. Tom had to laugh. He was jealous of William, but that wasn't why he didn't like him.

The warmth and brightness of the dorm greeted Tom like a long-lost friend. It would do him good to have an early night. He'd been working and worrying too much lately. Maybe he'd take a shower and then he and Danny could play some backgammon or watch TV. Tom hadn't spent much time with Danny lately either. He was missing Danny almost as much as he was missing Elizabeth.

Tom opened the door to his room, tensing instantly. The room was dark, but there was someone there—he could hear him breathing.

The first thing Tom thought of was the secret society. They were waiting for him. This was why they'd been so quiet; they were just biding their time. He flicked on the light switch and at the same time threw himself on the floor.

Laughter surrounded him.

Tom looked up. Danny and Isabella, curled up on Danny's bed, were laughing. They were laughing so much, the bed was shaking.

"You know, Tombo, I'm really beginning to worry about you," Danny said when he was finally able to speak. "You have got to learn to relax."

Elizabeth pulled up the hood of her parka as she stepped into the rainy night.

Ever since the beginning of the semester, the most Celine had ever done with any of her textbooks was take them to class and bring them back again. Sometimes she might move a book from the desk to the floor or, even more likely, from the floor to Elizabeth's bed, but she rarely did more than that. The only time Elizabeth had actually seen Celine open a book was when she was looking for a note or a shopping list that had been absentmindedly stuck between its pages. Tonight, however, Celine had decided to study. Someone must have accidentally told her that midterms were coming up, because it wasn't something she would have realized by herself. She had textbooks and notebooks spread across the floor of their room and a language cassette playing on Elizabeth's tape machine so she could study her French while she was studying her history, English, and math. She'd even gone out and bought a coffeemaker, which she'd balanced precariously on top of the pile of clothes on her desk.

"It'll be a miracle if she doesn't set the whole place on fire," Elizabeth commented as she pitched herself into the storm. She'd rather spend the rest of the evening sitting under a tree, waiting to be struck by lightning, than trying to get anything done with Celine thumping around, pretending to be a student.

Elizabeth continued talking to herself as she hurried away from Dickenson Hall. "It was probably Tom who told Celine it's exam time," she said. "He's the only friend she has who can read."

Celine and Tom—it really did make you wonder. Isabella was right. If Tom was the person he seemed to be, what interest could he have in Celine? Elizabeth had lived with Celine long enough to know that Celine was interested in only three things: herself, money, and power. She probably was more interested in herself than in money and power, but it was close. Elizabeth couldn't believe that even Wildman Watts would have wanted to go out with Celine.

Seeing that the lights were still on in the coffeehouse, Elizabeth decided to go in there. It was warm and dry, and she could sit at a corner table and pretend to be going over her English notes while she figured out what she was going to do about Jessica's invitation to dinner.

"I'd rather dine with Count Dracula than Mike McAllery," she told herself as she entered the café. The trouble was, she couldn't really say no. Jessica needed her. If Elizabeth refused to go to dinner, Mike might take it out on her sister. Elizabeth shuddered. The image of Jessica, crouched by the side of the bed, her face white with fear and her eyes swollen with tears after one of Mike McAllery's temper tantrums, wasn't going to leave her for a long, long time.

If only she could bring someone with her, it might not be so bad. At least she'd have an ally. But whom could she bring? Nina was out of the question, and so was William. There wasn't anyone else.

Because of the rain and the impending midterms, the coffeehouse was almost empty for a change. Elizabeth looked around the room. There was a couple with their heads bent over a book at one table and a couple of fraternity guys stuffing food into their faces at another. And there was Tom.

Elizabeth's heart did an unexpected leap. She'd been trying to talk to him for days, and now that she wasn't looking for him, there he was.

She came up behind him, touching his shoulder. "Tom."

He turned immediately, but the smile on his face was his polite, professional one.

"We meet at last," he joked. "When you didn't show up the other night, I started thinking you were still mad at me because of the secret society piece."

Elizabeth sat down across from him. "I am still mad at you," she said pleasantly. "But it doesn't matter what you think anymore, because I discovered who one of the leaders is."

He didn't question the suggestion that there was more than one. Instead he raised his eyebrows skeptically. "For sure?"

She nodded. "Absolutely for sure. There's not a doubt in my mind."

He tilted back his chair. "So?" he said, spreading out his hands. "Don't keep me in suspense, Elizabeth. Who is it?"

She rested her arms on the table. "Mike McAllery."

Tom didn't react. He continued to stare at her, his eyes giving nothing away. "Why?"

Elizabeth told him why.

Tom listened in silence while she explained her reasons, not interrupting her once. At the end of her story he was still silent, still showing no emotion.

"Well?" she asked. "Why don't you congratulate me? Why don't you help me decide what to do next?"

"Because I think you're totally out of your mind, that's why."

Elizabeth couldn't have been more surprised if he'd suddenly thrown his cup of tea at her. "What do you mean, you think I'm out of my mind? He's the perfect suspect and you know it. He—"

"He's a really nice guy," Tom cut in. "I happen to have a lot of time for Mike."

She must be dreaming. It was bad enough that Tom had suddenly taken to Celine, but Mike? What was wrong with Tom lately? If one of them had lost his or her mind, it wasn't Elizabeth, that was for sure.

"Oh, do you?" she snapped. "Well, isn't that great. The most violent, disreputable, shady, arrogant punk in Southern California, and you think he's a nice guy."

"I didn't say he was perfect, Elizabeth," Tom protested. "I just said I don't think he's our man. I like him."

There was no use in arguing with Tom, she knew that much. If she was going to change his mind about Mike, it would only be by showing him the truth about him.

And then it came to her. She could show Tom the real Mike *and* get through an evening with the McAllerys at the same time.

"Well, that's just perfect," she said, smiling the way Celine smiled—insincerely. "Then you won't mind having dinner with me, Mike, and Jess on Friday night."

Tom gave her a curious look, but he didn't ask for any explanation. "You're on," he said. "I could use a night out."

Chapter Five

Nina whacked the Ping-Pong ball across the table. "So what do you think?" she asked. "You and William want to double with me and Bryan for the charity ball?" She hit the ball back again, this time not so hard. "It should be quite a blast."

Elizabeth just managed to reach her shot, which at least gave her a few seconds before she had to answer. She wasn't sure what to say to Nina about the charity ball. Nothing would make Elizabeth happier than to double with Nina and Bryan. She was in favor of anything that raised money for a good cause, but personally, she'd rather write an article making people aware of what was going on than get dressed up and spend the night sipping champagne punch. William, however, was not only looking forward to the ball, he was insisting that they go alone.

"I'm really sorry, Nina, but I can't," Elizabeth panted as the ball came sailing back toward her. "William's one of the chairs, so we have to hang out with the organizers and smile a lot." A blast was the last thing it was going to be.

"He's one of the *chairs*?" The beads on Nina's braids rattled as she jumped for her shot. "Then maybe it's better you two aren't seen with us. Bryan and I are going to make a little statement at the ball."

"Make a statement?" Elizabeth ran to the corner to retrieve the ball. "But it's a charity do to raise money for inner-city kids to go to summer camp," she said, getting ready to serve. "Isn't that enough of a statement?"

"Not for Bryan." Nina grinned. "Not for me either," she added. "At first we were just going to buy our tickets and not go. Neither of us is really the glittering-social-organization kind of person. And it does seem sort of indecent to strut around in your best clothes, eating fancy canapés and drinking wine just because you've bought some poor kid a couple of weeks of sunshine and three square meals a day. But in the end we decided we could go after all and have a good time."

Elizabeth gave her a calculating look. "I'm almost afraid to ask how," she said. "You're not going to stage a picket outside or something, are you?"

Nina laughed. "Elizabeth, please, this isn't

the sixties. And besides, we aren't against the ball. We just want to make it a little more user-friendly."

"How friendly?"

"Well, the tickets do say you can bring a guest. So we're bringing some of the kids from Bryan's after-school project with us." She grinned impishly. "We thought everybody might like to actually meet some of the children they're trying to help."

Elizabeth tested the paddle in her hand. She had the feeling that there were going to be quite a few people at the ball who weren't even remotely interested in meeting the objects of their charity face-to-face. She could imagine Alison Quinn, vice president of the Thetas, the campus's most prestigious and snobbish sorority, confronted with real kids from the inner city. A disloyal little voice deep in her mind whispered that William White was very likely to be one of those people, too.

"There are a lot of things in my life that I don't understand right now," Elizabeth said, "but at least now there's one thing I'm pretty clear on." She got ready for her serve.

"And what's that?" asked Nina.

"I now understand why everyone thinks Bryan Nelson's a troublemaker."

"He's not a troublemaker," Nina protested immediately. "He's—"

Elizabeth laughed. "I didn't say I agreed with them, Nina; I just said I understood." The ball left her hand and streaked through the air. "Personally, now that I know what you two are planning, I'm really looking forward to it."

William's not going to think it's so funny, said that disloyal little voice again. Elizabeth slammed the ball against the far wall.

Winston was sitting in a far corner of the snack bar, absorbed in a magazine he was reading. It was a women's magazine. He'd seen it in the bookstore and bought it on impulse because of the title of one of the articles listed on the front: "How Can He Tell What You're Thinking?"

Winston put the magazine down with a sigh of defeat. "He can't," he said, picking up his soda. "He doesn't have any idea what you're thinking, and nobody's going to tell him, either."

He sighed again. Winston had hoped that the article might give him some useful advice on figuring out what went on inside a woman's head, but this was clearly a secret piece of information that no women's magazine was prepared to reveal. All he'd learned from the article was that every man since the beginning of time had trouble understanding the opposite sex.

"Poor Adam," Winston mumbled. "He

probably only ate the apple because he thought it would make Eve happy."

Winston looked around the room at the smiling couples sitting close together at other tables. How had they first gotten together? How had that guy with the big ears and the goofy smile known that the pretty girl sitting with her head on his shoulder, reading a newspaper, was interested in him? How had the girl with the orange hair and the ring through her nose known that the guy with the buzz cut and the tattoo on his wrist really cared?

It was a mystery to him. Winston got up to get himself an order of fries, leaving his book bag and the open magazine on the table so no one would take his seat. All this anxiety was giving him an appetite. One minute he was sure that Denise liked him as more than a friend, and the next he was sure that she didn't.

"I can't go on like this," Winston mumbled to himself as he bumped into a display of tea bags. "I'm an emotional yo-yo. I can't concentrate on anything, I'm losing sleep—"

The guy in front of him turned around. "Did you say something?"

Winston shook his head. *And I'm talking to myself in public.* How much worse could it get? What was going to happen to him?

While he waited for a fresh batch of fries to be made, Winston thought about what was going to happen to him if he went on like this. He'd fail his midterms because he hadn't been able to get his mind off Denise long enough to think about logarithms or William Shakespeare. His professors would start banning him from his classes because he talked to himself all the time and disturbed the other students. With nothing to do, Winston would shuffle around the campus, talking to himself. He'd spend all his money on women's magazines. The college authorities would become concerned. They'd contact his parents. His parents would send him to a rest home in the desert, where he'd learn to do beadwork and play bridge. He'd never finish college or make anything of himself. He'd spend the rest of his life sitting in the sun stringing tiny bits of colored plastic, and all because he hadn't been able to figure out if Denise Waters wanted to go out with him or not.

Winston was almost back at his seat before he realized that someone else had sat down in it and was reading his magazine.

Denise looked up as he tripped over his feet and banged into the table.

"Have you been holding out on me, Winnie?" she asked, flapping the magazine in his face.

Holding out on her? Holding what out on her? Winston grunted, but he was too surprised to speak.

Denise cocked her head to one side, looking

watchful. "Come on," she coaxed. "I'm practically your best friend. You can tell me."

The news that Denise was practically his best friend made Winston's heart want to leave home. "There isn't anything to tell you, Denise," he managed to choke out. "Really."

She was still watching him. "Just tell me if it's okay if I sit with you, then. I'm not going to be interrupting something, am I?"

"Interrupting something?" Winston collapsed in the chair beside her, wondering what she was talking about.

She nodded. "Yes, interrupting something." She gave him a kick. "You know, Win, *interrupting something*."

Winston stared back at her in horror as he suddenly realized what she meant. She thought he was sitting with someone else; another girl. A girl who read women's magazines. "Well, no, I— No, it's—" he stumbled. "No, of course you're not interrupting anything."

Denise helped herself to a fry. "So where is she?" she asked.

"Where is who?" He should have gotten two orders of fries. His stress level was already rising.

"Where is the girl who owns this magazine?"

"There is no girl," Winston said. "It's mine."

Denise grinned. *"Yours?"* The grin became a laugh. "Since when do you read things like this?"

"That magazine happens to have some very interesting articles in it, Denise. Very educational." He stuffed a handful of fries in his mouth to stop himself from talking.

"Oh, right," Denise said. She looked down at the cover and then back at him. "So what were you finding so educational?" she asked. "'Twenty Days to a Flatter Tummy' or 'Cystitis and You'?"

"Dinner's ready!" Steven called into the living room. He spooned the drained pasta into a bowl and poured the sauce he'd made over it.

"Mmmm . . ." Billie said appreciatively as she came into the kitchen. "That smells great. I'm sure glad one of us can cook Italian food."

Steven put the steaming dish on the table. "You know what I can't get over?" he asked her as he went back for the salad.

Billie sat down. "If we're talking about Mike McAllery again, you can't get over the fact that he had the nerve to think you would sit in the same room with him and share a meal." She broke off a piece of garlic bread.

"No, besides that." Steven sat across from her. "Do you know what else I can't get over?"

Billie closed her eyes as she bit into her bread. "This is wonderful," she mumbled. "I think I could live on garlic bread if I had to. Garlic bread and spaghetti."

She couldn't fool him; she was pretending to ignore him. She didn't want to talk about Mike McAllery anymore, so she was going to spend the entire meal talking about garlic bread and spaghetti. But Steven did want to talk about Mike, and he wasn't going to be put off.

"I can't get over the fact that Jessica and Mike actually have people over to dinner. I mean, doesn't it seem strange to you, Billie? It's so *normal*. It's the kind of thing you and I do, or my parents do. It's not the kind of thing a thug who rides a souped-up motorcycle does."

Billie smacked her lips together softly. "What is this in the sauce? Capers? Anchovies?" She took another mouthful. "It really is delicious, Steven. Even better than last time."

Steven knew exactly what Billie was thinking. She was thinking that if she complimented him on his sauce, he'd get distracted and forget about the fact that Mike and Jessica had dinner parties. But Steven couldn't forget about it. It had been bothering him ever since he left Mike standing in front of that garage. Because he disliked Mike so much, Steven had never really given much thought to what he and Jessica did when they were together. Now he couldn't stop wondering and imagining.

Steven slowly twisted several strands of spaghetti onto his fork. "Billie, what do you think they do together?"

Billie stopped chewing and staring at him as though she hadn't realized he was sitting there. "Do?" she repeated. "What do I think who does together?"

"Jess and the caveman."

"What do you mean, *do*? Are you accusing Mike of unnatural sexual practices? Do you think he dresses in a wet suit and makes Jessica message him with rubber ducks or something?"

Steven felt his face turn red. Where did Billie get this stuff? From women's magazines? "Of course I don't mean that," he snapped. "I mean *do*. You know, when they're just hanging out together. Do you think they go bowling and stuff like that?"

"How do I know if they go bowling? Sure, I guess. Why wouldn't they?"

"I just can't picture Mike doing things like that, that's all. I mean, do you think they watch television and play Scrabble and order from the Chinese place down the street?"

Billie put down her fork and rested her chin on her hands. "No," she said. "I don't think Jess and Mike do anything like that. I don't think they cook together, or go shopping, or do the laundry, or listen to music. I think they swing from the ceiling on chains and eat lightbulbs and nails."

Steven helped himself to salad. "I don't see what you're getting so sarcastic about. Even you'd have to admit that McAllery isn't like the rest of us. How do I know what someone like that considers ordinary domestic life?"

The way she grabbed her fork, he almost thought she was going to stab him with it. "What is wrong with you, Steven? Mike McAllery is a human being, just like you are. He does the same things you do when he's at home, except he probably doesn't leave his socks on the floor."

"You think he cooks?" Steven asked. He couldn't picture Mike McAllery in his leather jacket, cooking. That was too much. He probably ate his meat raw.

"Why not?" Billie demanded. "What's so strange about that? He might be a great cook. He might even be a better cook than you are."

"He can't be," Steven said. After all, Mike McAllery was a mechanic and Steven was a sophisticated, educated prelaw student. How could Mike McAllery be a better cook than he was?

Billie smiled at him. There was something just a little hostile about her smile. "I'll tell you one thing I bet he's good at," she said. "I bet he gives Jessica incredible backrubs. You can see it in his hands."

Steven blushed again. "Billie, please. I'm trying to eat. I don't want to think about Mike rubbing Jessica's back when I'm trying to eat."

"You're the one who brought it up," Billie said.

Mark raised his wineglass over the pale-green linen tablecloth. "Eat, drink, and be merry!" he toasted. "For tomorrow you may die."

Alex clinked her glass against his, resisting the temptation simply to throw it at him. She'd talked Mark into going out to dinner because there was nothing he liked better than a big meal in a fancy restaurant. She thought they might be able to recapture the fun they'd had when they first dated, but it was becoming all too apparent that if she wanted to recapture those days, she should have taken a video.

"That's not very cheery," she said, hiding her annoyance in a pleasant smile. "I thought we were going to really enjoy ourselves tonight."

Mark sneered. "Oh, sure," he said. "The condemned man had a terrific time."

Alex ground her teeth together. The condemned man wasn't going to live long enough to reach the gas chamber at the rate he was going. He was going to be stabbed to death with a seafood fork in one of the county's swankiest restaurants if he wasn't careful.

Still trying to be patient and supportive, Alex lifted her glass again. "What about the future?" she suggested. "Someday this will all be behind you, you know. It'll be like none of this ever happened. Why don't we forget about all the garbage that's going on now and toast the future?"

116

Much to her amazement, this suggestion seemed to meet with Mark's approval. In fact, it even seemed to cheer him up.

"That's more like it!" he cried, swinging his glass into the air with such force that some of the wine splashed over the table. "Let's toast tomorrow, when Mark Gathers is a pro superstar with a mansion in Hollywood Hills and a customized Porsche Cerrera." For the first time in days he smiled at her with something of the old charm and affection. "You're right, Alex," he said. "I'm the one who's going to have the last laugh. Maybe my career at SVU is over, but that doesn't mean I'm not going to make it big. I'm still one of the best basketball players in California. Nothing the dean and his stupid committee do is going to change that."

Also for the first time in days, Alex felt something close to hope flow through her. Maybe things were going to be all right between her and Mark after all. They would weather this storm and come out on the other side, stronger and more together than ever. Instead of treating her like his mother, he would treat her the way he used to, as though she was the most beautiful and desirable woman in the world. He would compliment her all the time instead of complaining that she was nagging him.

"That's right," she said, their glasses clinking. "You're going to show them all."

He nodded. "I am, Alex. I really am. I'm going to be the best player this country's ever seen. I'm going to do TV commercials and guest appearances on 'The Tonight Show.' The women will be after me in droves." He was smiling at her, but he was looking into the future at how rich and famous he was going to be. "Maybe I'll even cut a record," he continued, lost in his fantasy. "Everywhere I go, people will follow me, wanting my autograph or just to touch my arm. I won't have any peace." He drank a sip of wine, his expression dreamy. "I bet I'll look back on nights like this, when I could just sit in a restaurant like an ordinary person, with real nostalgia . . ."

Alex picked up her menu, hiding behind it while she blinked back a tear. She hadn't heard anything that suggested she might be driving around in his Porsche with him. But why should he want her there? He was going to have droves of women chasing after him. As another tear threatened to run down her cheek, Alex decided to change the subject.

"Since you don't have to do 'The Tonight Show' in the next week or two, what about the charity ball? Have you decided whether you want to go or not?"

The smile left his face and his eyes became troubled again. "Are you nuts, Alex?" He took another swallow of wine. "I can't go to that.

I'm trying to keep a low profile." He picked up his menu and started to study it. "You go without me."

Alex stared at her own menu, but it might as well have been blank. *I guess I will have to go without you,* she told him silently. *Since you seem to be going without me.*

Jessica stopped at the entrance to El Capitano, one of the most expensive restaurants in California, if not the whole world, glancing nervously over at Mike. He looked even more gorgeous than usual, all dressed up in a pale-gray suit, dark-gray silk shirt, and wine-red tie.

"Are you really sure you want to go here?" she asked. "We could go somewhere else."

"I know we could go somewhere else," Mike answered as he propelled her past the doorman and into the elegantly understated interior of the restaurant. "But you like this place, so this is where we're eating."

Mike had a new campaign going to make her happy. He thought that the problem between them was that she was feeling a little lonely and isolated because his lifestyle was so different from what she was used to, so he was trying to make it up to her by doing things he thought she enjoyed. He'd even volunteered to take her bowling, though she already knew that would be pretty much his idea of spending an evening in hell.

"I really don't mind," Jessica protested, trying to stop him from walking so fast. She already wished she'd never mentioned El Capitano. The truth was that she didn't know whether she liked it or she didn't like it, since she'd never been here before. She only knew of it because it was a favorite with the Thetas, her old sorority. Alison Quinn was always going on about how wonderful El Capitano was and how it catered to only the most sophisticated tastes. So when Mike asked her where she wanted to go for dinner, Jessica blurted, "El Capitano," before she realized that it was exactly the kind of place Mike hated most. He might look like a rock star having a night out, he might be able to get them one of the best tables in the place without blinking an eye, and he could certainly afford the exorbitant prices, but Jessica knew that Mike felt much happier in diners than in restaurants like this. He hated pretension and he hated snobs.

Well, we've certainly come to the right place for pretentious snobs, Jessica thought as they followed the waiter across the tiled floor. There was a large table of Thetas and Sigmas sitting squarely in the middle of the room, laughing and posing as though they thought they were being filmed. Jessica refused to meet their eyes as they passed them, but she was sure she saw two of them exchange a smirk.

Mike didn't notice. Mike was too busy taking in the mock-Spanish decor and the number of mink coats casually draped over the backs of chairs. "I guess they don't do beans and rice in this place," he commented as they sat down at their table.

Jessica didn't answer. Her attention had been caught by a couple across the room from them. It was Alexandra Rollins and Mark Gathers, looking as at home in El Capitano as a king and queen on their thrones.

After he'd pushed in Jessica's chair, the waiter passed Mike the wine list. "Not for me," Mike said. "Maybe my wife would like some wine, but I'll just have a beer."

Jessica stifled a groan. One definitely didn't groan audibly in El Capitano. Mike noticed anyway.

"What's the matter?" he asked as the waiter shimmied off for a bottle of beer and a bottle of mineral water. "What'd I do now?"

"You ordered beer!" she hissed. "I don't believe you. You can't order beer in a place like this."

Mike looked puzzled. "Why not? They serve it."

Don't get on his case, she warned herself. *He's trying to please you. The least you can do is have a good time.* "You're right," she said, giving him one of her warmest smiles. "Of course they serve it. I might even have a little sip of yours myself."

121

"Oh no, you don't," he teased, starting to read the menu. "I'll share everything I've got with you, baby, but not my beer. You can get your own."

Jessica cringed inwardly. The Thetas already thought she was beneath their contempt because she lived with Mike and had worked in the coffeehouse. She didn't need for them to see her drinking beer in El Capitano, too.

"I hope the food's good," Mike said as he read through the menu.

"Of course the food's good," Jessica said. "This place gets written up everywhere."

"That doesn't mean the food's good," he answered. He gave her a smile. "Anyway, no matter how many write-ups they get, this meal isn't going to be as good as the one you're making tomorrow."

Jessica smiled back at him, wondering how he could be so confident in her ability to throw a dinner party when she wasn't confident at all.

"What are you making?" he asked.

Jessica had been praying he wouldn't ask that question. She'd been through so many magazines and recipe books that she was going slightly insane. Every time she made her mind up on one thing, she saw something else that seemed either easier or better. She'd changed the menu ten times in the last day alone, and she still had no idea what she was going to make.

"It's a secret," she said. "You'll have to wait to find out just like everybody else."

"Aw, come on, baby," he wheedled, "that's not fair. I'm really excited about this. I want to know what you're making. You know I'd help if I didn't have to have that Buick done by five o'clock."

She'd been counting on his help. Mike wasn't only a fantastic cook, he was the kind of cook who made it look easy. Jessica was the kind of cook who made it look hard. "No, don't beg me. I want it to be a surprise."

"Tamales?" he asked hopefully. Tamales were one of Mike's favorite things.

Jessica's eyes fell on Alex and Mark again. They were drinking wine and gazing into each other's eyes. Not for the first time, Jessica wondered how things could have turned out the way they had. There was Alex, ex-dork Enid Rollins, now a Theta sister with a superjock boyfriend and a glamorous life, and here was Jessica, the undisputed queen of Sweet Valley High, discussing tamales with a man who drank beer from the bottle.

"Will you tell me if I guess it?"

"No." She picked up her menu and hid behind it. "What is this?" she demanded, peering over the edge of the glossy black leather. "It isn't in English."

"Of course not," Mike said. "It's in Spanish." The waiter materialized beside them with their drinks. It seemed to Jessica that he was looking at them with a certain amount of distaste. "I can translate if you need help," he offered in a patronizing tone.

Mike shook his head. "That's all right; I read Spanish."

Jessica felt a surge of pride. Maybe this evening would turn out all right after all.

"But I don't drink beer from a glass, so you can take this back."

And maybe it wouldn't.

"I really can't stay long, Danny," Tom was saying as Danny shoved him through the door of the coffeehouse. "I've got—"

"I know, I know, you've got a lot of work to do." He led the way to an empty table. "But you've always got a lot of work to do. If I listen to that crap, I never see you."

Tom followed Danny through the dimly lit café. A jazz quartet was playing on the tiny stage, giving the place a warm, relaxed atmosphere. Tom began to relax slightly himself. He really hadn't wanted to come, but Danny had practically dragged him out of the station.

Once again Tom had been going through the material Elizabeth and he had gathered on the fraternities, as well as the little they'd been able to find on the secret society itself, looking for a clue to the leader's identity. There had to be one—one tiny, easy-to-miss clue—but Tom couldn't seem to find it no matter how hard he tried.

I'm being blind, he told himself as he sat down next to Danny. *I bet it's right in front of my eyes and I'm not seeing it.* Which at least was a change from Elizabeth, who was seeing things that weren't there.

"You eat tonight?" Danny asked.

Tom wasn't sure if he'd even eaten today, but he wasn't going to tell Danny that. Danny was going through one of his worried-about-Tom phases, when he was always after Tom to eat or sleep or ask Elizabeth Wakefield out. Tom found these phases exhausting. "I grabbed something earlier," he lied.

Danny knew he was lying. "They've got some good specials tonight," Danny said, looking at the blackboard on the wall behind Tom. "Black bean soup . . . broccoli quiche . . ."

Black bean soup didn't sound so bad. Tom turned around to see what the other specials were, and immediately wished that he hadn't. Instead of not seeing something that was there, he was seeing something that he wished weren't there—Celine Boudreaux, all dressed up as though she were going to a fancy party.

He turned back to Danny. "Now look what you've gotten me into," he muttered. "Celine's coming over."

125

"Of all the coffeehouses in all the world . . ." Danny mumbled, but he didn't look any happier than Tom felt.

"Tom!" He could feel the hair on the back of his neck stand up. "Tom, sugar, I'm so glad I ran into you. I am in the most foul mood." She plopped into the seat beside him.

Danny shot to his feet. "If you two will excuse me for a minute—" He waved his hand, giving the impression that he was going to the john, but Tom knew better. Danny was going to hide until Tom got rid of Celine.

Celine, who hadn't seemed to notice that Danny was with Tom, certainly didn't notice that he'd left. She put her head on Tom's shoulder, pouting seductively.

"Can you believe it, sugar? I've been stood up. Stood up. Me!" She ruffled the gold taffeta skirt she was wearing. "Look at me—here I am all dolled up to go to El Capitano with Peter and his Sigma buddies and he has to go to some hush-hush meeting at the last minute instead."

While Celine had been talking and getting makeup all over the shoulder of his shirt, Tom had been trying to think of a way to get rid of her quickly and efficiently. Something short of murder but just as effective. At the words "hush-hush meeting," however, he stopped thinking. It wasn't a Sigma meeting if Celine and Peter had been planning to go out with

126

Peter's pals. If it wasn't a Sigma meeting, what kind of meeting could it be? *I wonder,* Tom said to himself. *I really, really wonder.*

He leaned back so that his face was so close to Celine's they might be about to kiss. If he wasn't mistaken, Celine had been drowning her disappointment in a glass of wine or two.

"You're kidding," he said, sounding indignant even to his own ears. "Peter stood you up?" He made a face. "What meeting could be more important than you, Celine?"

Celine pressed against him. "That's what I'd like to know. Peter and his secret this and secret that; you'd think he was running the CIA or something the way he carries on." She kicked the table leg with one gold lamé shoe. "He thinks he's hot stuff, Peter Wilbourne, but believe me, he isn't."

Tom could hardly believe his luck. All the hours he'd spent trying to woo Celine and get some information out of her, and here she was, showing all the fury of a woman scorned—and the effects of a little wine—and finally about to tell him something he wanted to know. He was sure she was; he could feel it in his bones.

Celine cuddled a little closer. "Of course, I shouldn't be complaining to you about Peter, should I, Tommy?" she asked, the anger instantly dissolved from her voice.

I don't care, Tom wanted to say. *Complain*

127

all you want. But he could tell that she was through with that now. She wasn't interested in Peter anymore. She was interested in him.

She touched his knee with hers. "And anyway," she drawled, "he's done us a favor, hasn't he? I mean, if I'd gone with Peter, then I wouldn't have run into you."

Tom's eyes searched the doorway Danny had disappeared through. Why wasn't he coming back? He wasn't really going to leave Tom with Celine all night, was he? Whatever happened to male bonding and loyalty between friends?

"Maybe we should go somewhere else," Celine suggested the way a cat might suggest a walk into the corner to a mouse. "Somewhere we could get a little wine and a little privacy, maybe." She pushed his hair back, putting her lips to his ear. "I'm thirsty, Tommy, and I need a little affection."

"I wonder what happened to Danny," Tom said in desperation. He'd definitely blown it. She wasn't going to tell him anything now. How could he have been so close and ended up so far away? He laughed nervously. "Maybe he went with Peter to his meeting."

Celine rolled her eyes. "Believe me, they wouldn't let Danny into one of Peter's meetings."

Tom's heart gave a leap. *Don't push it*, he cautioned himself. *Take it easy*.

"Oh, so it's a Sigma meeting," he said, putting an arm around her. "Well, you can't blame him for having to go to that, Celine. He is the president of the fraternity. He'll have to run it."

"He's not running this meeting," Celine said, seeming to melt into his arms. "This isn't baby Sigma business; this is serious. The guy in charge of this meeting really could run the CIA."

Did she know any more? Did she have any idea who the leader was? He looked down at the honey-blond head. There was only one way to find out. "Come on," he said, straightening up. "Let's go see about getting you a little wine and a little affection."

Chapter Six

Elizabeth slept badly and woke up early. *Friday,* she thought as soon as her eyes were open. *D day.* D for dinner. *Or for disaster,* she added as she hurled herself out of bed. *Or doom. D for dining with the devil.*

All night long Elizabeth had woken up every hour or so, and every time she woke up, she thought: *How am I going to get out of going to Jess and Mike's?*

She was still wondering how she was going to get out of going as she gathered her shower things and headed for the bathroom. She banged into an empty stall and turned the faucets on full.

"It's not bad enough that I have to spend an entire evening pretending not to loathe the very sight of Mike McAllery, but I had to go and invite Tom along," Elizabeth fumed as the hot water poured down on her. "I must have been temporarily insane or something," she continued. "It's because he made me so angry, refusing to believe the truth about Mike, that's why. If he hadn't made me so angry, I never would have invited him."

She grabbed the loofah and scrubbed hard.

"I can't go to Jess's with Tom," she told the bar of soap. "I don't know how I'm going to get out of it, but I can't possibly go with him. We're not even really friends anymore. We don't go anywhere together, we don't do anything together. I mean, I've never even had a hamburger alone with him. What kind of support is he going to be? This is going to be one of the most gruesome ordeals of my entire life. I don't need someone who does nothing but argue with me by my side."

She reached for the shampoo.

"But even if I just tell Tom that he's not coming after all, then what? Then I'll be completely alone with Mike and Jess. I don't want to be alone with them. Even Tom would be better than nothing. Not much better, maybe, but better."

She must have used too much shampoo, because it went into her eyes.

Elizabeth groaned. "Oh, great, now I'm going to be blind. At least I won't have to look at either of them."

Someone tapped on the door of the shower.

"What?" Elizabeth shouted.

"Are you alone in there, Elizabeth?" Nina called back. Even through the running water Elizabeth could tell that Nina was trying unsuccessfully not to laugh.

"Of course I'm alone in here."

"Only checking," Nina said. She gave up trying not to laugh. "It's just that people usually sing in the shower, not argue."

Elizabeth reached for the faucets. *Those are people whose brother-in-laws don't come straight from hell.*

"Who opened the curtains?" Celine moaned as she struggled to pry her eyes open. "What's Princess Perfect trying to do, blind me?" One arm over her eyes to protect them, Celine reached for the curtains and tugged them closed.

"That's better," she said with a sigh as she collapsed back on her pillow. "Maybe I'll be all right if I just lie still for a while."

It was hard for her to think because her head felt as if it was about to rip itself apart, but as much as she could, Celine tried to remember what had happened last night.

"I went out," she told herself. "I went out with Peter."

She cautiously opened one eye and aimed it at the foot of her bed. Her gold party dress was

133

thrown across the footboard. So far, so good.

She closed both eyes again. Peter had arranged to meet her for a drink before they left for the restaurant, and that was when he told her that they weren't going to El Capitano after all. He didn't care that she'd bought a new dress just for the occasion. He didn't care that she was probably the only person of any real class and breeding who had never been there. He didn't care that he had ruined her evening. "It's not my fault, babe," he kept saying over and over. "This isn't something I can get out of. This isn't a meeting of the Boy Scouts; this is serious."

Carefully opening her eyes again, Celine reached over for a cigarette. It wasn't going to make her feel any better, but it probably wouldn't make her feel much worse, either.

Peter had been a little tipsy already, she remembered. That was why he'd been so indiscreet about where he was going—and why he'd told her more about the secret society than he should have. "If I don't show up, my whole future life will be in the toilet, babe," he'd assured her. "Is that what you want? You want me to end up in some dead-end job making peanuts when if I keep these guys happy, I can have everything I want?"

Celine blew a smoke ring across the room. Of course she hadn't wanted that. Peter without money and prestige would be about as interesting as a garden snail. But that hadn't stopped her from being really mad at him.

She took another drag. What had she done after Peter staggered off to his big important meeting?

Tom. After Peter left her, she went looking for Tom. And as sure as the Lord made water moccasins, she found him.

Celine groaned. How indiscreet had she been? She could remember running into Tom in the coffeehouse very clearly. She could remember cuddling against him and telling him what a louse Peter was. She remembered Tom saying, "Let's go get you a little wine and a little affection." She remembered having another glass of wine, but she certainly didn't remember getting any affection from Tom.

Celine sat up, stabbing her cigarette out in the ashtray. What had she said to Tom about the secret society? She'd been so angry, she might have said anything.

She reached for another cigarette with a philosophical shrug. What did it matter how much she said? She didn't know much. And if it got back to whoever it was who ran this hush-hush society, well, it wasn't Celine who was going to get into trouble. It was Peter. She smiled as she struck the match. Just what he deserved for ruining her night.

* * *

Elizabeth stared vacantly at the untouched salad in front of her. *One thing's for sure*, she told herself. *The My-Sister-Is-Married-to-a-Criminal diet is a lot more effective than any of the other diets I've tried.* In fact, the jeans she'd gotten several weeks ago to accommodate the weight she'd gained were practically falling off.

She pushed the plate away from her. Who could eat when they had so much to worry about? She didn't know what she was going to do tonight, when her twin would expect her to enjoy the dinner she'd made. *If only they had a dog*, Elizabeth thought. *Then at least I could pass it to him under the table.*

"If it isn't my favorite beautiful blonde," said a voice right beside her. "You're just the girl I was hoping to see."

Elizabeth looked up. Winston Egbert was standing over her with a tray that held enough food to feed Elizabeth for two days.

"Are you going to eat all that or are you expecting company?" she teased as he sat down across from her.

Winston picked up his first sandwich. "I'm stressed," he told her. "I always eat when I'm stressed. I get it from my mother."

"What's wrong?" Elizabeth asked, relieved to get her mind off her own problems for a while. "Are you worried about midterms?"

"Nothing that simple," Winston mumbled

through a mouthful of tuna salad on rye. "I'm worried about women."

Elizabeth felt the first smile of the day come over her face. "Worried about women? Why, do you think they're trying to steal your onion rings?"

Winston shook his head. "That's just it, Elizabeth. I don't know what to think about them. I can't figure women out." He grabbed a couple of fries. "That's why I was hoping to run into you. I need your advice."

It was a good thing it was so much easier to give advice to other people than it was to yourself. "Go ahead," Elizabeth said. "What is it?"

"Okay, this is the question," Winston said, leaning so far over the table that his shirt dipped into the mustard on his onion rings. "How can a guy tell when a girl really likes him?" He waggled a french fry in her direction. "You know, Elizabeth, *really* likes him."

Elizabeth stared at him, trying to think of some response that wasn't laughter. Why was he asking her? There'd been times in the last months when she was sure Tom Watts really liked her, but she'd been totally wrong. She'd even thought he'd written her a poem—she'd been sure of it—only to find out that it was William who wrote it.

"I think you may have come to the wrong person," Elizabeth finally answered. "I'm not

137

sure I can always tell myself when somebody really likes me."

Winston took up his sandwich again. "But you're a woman, Elizabeth. You must know. There must be signs you give . . ."

She rested her arms on the edge of the table. "Are we talking about a specific woman, Winston, or is this just a general question?"

"Specific," he quickly replied. His face turned the color of the slice of tomato that he'd dropped on his shirt.

The dimple appeared in Elizabeth's left cheek. "Denise Waters specific?" she guessed.

He nodded. "It's driving me nuts, Elizabeth, it really is. If I don't work this out soon, my food bill will bankrupt me."

"But you know Denise likes you," Elizabeth said. When Winston was pledging the Sigmas and having so much trouble with hazing, Denise had been so concerned she'd come to Elizabeth for help.

Winston sighed as he chewed. "Yeah, I know she likes me, Elizabeth. But does she *really* like me? I mean, we do a lot of things together, and she'll put her arm in mine when we're walking and stuff like that, but how can I tell if she wants to be more than pals?"

Elizabeth frowned. Could Tom tell that she *really* liked him even though she was dating William? Was he able to read her signals? Had she given him any? Well, there was one way Tom could find out, if he wanted to know. "Why don't you just ask her?"

"Ask her?" Winston gaped at Elizabeth as though she'd suggested flinging himself out the window. "Are you kidding? You want me to *ask* her?"

"It is a pretty sure way of finding out."

"It's also a pretty sure way of being rejected in person." Winston jammed another fistful of fries into his mouth.

"But what's the use of torturing yourself, Winston, when all you have to do is say, 'Denise, what are your true feelings for me—I have to know'?"

"Because what if her true feelings for me are the same as the ones she has for her dog? What if she likes having me around but she doesn't want me up on the bed?"

"But at least you'd *know*," Elizabeth protested.

Winston picked up his second sandwich. "I don't want to know if she's going to dump me," he said. "I'd rather live in hope."

Out of the corner of her eye Elizabeth saw a familiar dark figure in a blue ski jacket, so handsome he took her breath away, hurry out of the cafeteria with a cup of coffee in his hand. Tom.

I guess maybe I would, too, she thought.

* * *

Just don't let me run into Steven right now, Jessica pleaded silently as she lugged her heavy shopping bags into the foyer of her apartment building. *If he starts yelling at me, I might clobber him with broccoli.*

Jessica slowly climbed the stairs. She'd done exactly what the article she'd found called "Your First Dinner Party" had instructed her to do. She'd chosen her menu. She'd made a list of everything she needed. She'd gone to the supermarket, her list clutched tightly in her hand, and she'd methodically gone from one aisle to the next.

The article, though, hadn't said what you did when the store was out of some of the things you needed. Jessica wasn't quite sure herself what a shallot was, but Foodland didn't have any. She changed the menu from chicken with shallots to chicken with mushrooms.

The avocados were all as hard as rocks. She changed the appetizer from corn chips and guacamole to potato chips and sour cream dip. She wasn't sure what cilantro was, either, so she bought parsley instead.

Jessica had planned to cheat a little on the first course by buying a couple of containers of Mrs. Marin's Homemade Carrot Soup, but Foodland didn't carry anything by Mrs. Marin. She bought some carrots. How hard could soup be to make?

The salad called for walnuts, but there must have been a rush on shelled walnuts, because she couldn't find any. She bought them with shells.

There wasn't any more French bread or chocolate-chip brownies in the bakery. She bought bake-and-serve rolls and chocolate ice cream. All she'd done so far for this evening's meal was buy the ingredients, and already she was exhausted.

Gasping for breath, Jessica pushed open the apartment door and staggered inside. "Oh, no!" she moaned, looking around with a sinking heart. Somehow, in her rush to get to her first class this morning, she'd totally forgotten about the state of the house. There were piles of magazines and newspapers all over the floor of the living room. From where she was standing, she could see a pair of Mike's socks under the sofa and the blue bowl she'd been looking for last night, with a spoon still in it.

"Food first," she decided, hauling the groceries into the kitchen. "Once I get dinner started, I can straighten out the living room." She threw her jacket into the corner. "And then I can take a nice hot bubble bath and relax before they get here." At least she'd already picked out what she was wearing—a long, slim tapestry vest over a short swingy black skirt. She was going to look fantastic. Even Elizabeth would

141

have to admire Jessica's ability to present a meal worthy of a professional chef *and* look like a model at the same time.

Jessica got out her cookbooks and rolled up her sleeves. It was four o'clock.

By five o'clock she'd discovered just how hard it was to make carrot soup. There were two scorched saucepans in the sink and several blobs of something that looked like baby food on the kitchen floor.

"I'll do something with the soup later," she decided. "I'll make the salad now. That shouldn't be hard." She couldn't find a nutcracker.

By six o'clock Jessica had discovered that a hammer wasn't really a perfect substitute for a nutcracker. If you held the walnut still, there was a very good chance you would hit your own fingers. If you didn't hold the walnut still, there was an even better chance that the walnut would skid across the room.

At six thirty Jessica remembered the chicken.

"Oh, my gosh!" she shrieked. "The chicken! How could I forget the chicken?" She wasn't sure how long it took to make chicken and mushrooms, but Elizabeth and Tom were coming at eight. If it took as long as half an hour to get the thing into the oven, she'd only have just enough time to blitz the living room and have her bath.

Wash the chicken pieces and pat dry, the recipe

instructed. *Heat three tablespoons of olive oil in a large skillet. Sauté the garlic and shallots until golden. Set aside. Add the chicken to the oil in the pan, browning on all sides.*

Jessica didn't have time for sautéing this and browning that. She poured some oil into the frying pan and dumped the chicken and the mushrooms in together. While they were cooking, she raced into the living room and started stuffing things into drawers and closets and under the cushions on the couch.

At seven o'clock the smoke alarm went off. Jessica looked up from fishing a pair of her tights from behind the television set to see a cloud of smoke drifting out of the kitchen. This was all she needed. The chicken was on fire.

Jessica skidded into the kitchen, coughing and trying to see through the smoke. The chicken really was on fire: sharp orange flames were dancing around the rim of the pan. She turned off the burner, but she couldn't remember what you were supposed to do for kitchen fires. Should she throw the whole thing in the sink? Find a fire extinguisher, maybe?

The fire alarm in the bedroom went off, too. The smoke was advancing. Jessica collapsed on the kitchen floor and burst into tears.

The first she knew that Mike was home was when she heard him shout, "What the hell's going on in here?" The front door slammed.

143

"Baby?" he shouted, fighting his way through the smoke. "Baby, what happened?" He scooped her into his arms. "Jess, are you all right?"

"I'm a failure," she sobbed. "I'm a failure as a wife. Elizabeth is going to be here in less than an hour and there won't be anything to eat, and the house is a mess, and—"

"You're not a failure. You're the most wonderful wife in the world." He kissed her till she was quiet, holding her tight. "I'll tell you what. Why don't you go take a nice hot bath and I'll clean up this mess?"

"But what about dinner?" Jessica wailed. "Everything's ruined. The only thing we have to eat is potato chips."

"I'll call that Tex-Mex place on Salceda Avenue. They do great enchiladas."

"But there won't be enough time."

"Sure, there'll be time. You go take a bath, baby. I'll take care of everything."

Just as she reached the doorway he called her back. "Can I ask you just one tiny little question, Jess, without you starting to cry again?"

"Sure," she snuffled.

"What are all these walnuts doing on the floor?"

The only light on in the WSVU office came from the small lamp beside Tom's computer. Tom sat with his feet up on the desk and his eyes closed, going over and over last night's encounter with Celine in his mind. He'd intended to take her back to her dorm when they left the coffee-house, but she'd insisted on getting more wine. "You promised," she kept saying, clinging to him so hard she practically choked him. "You're not like the others, are you, Tom? Aren't you a man who always keeps his promises?"

Not always, he felt like saying, but this time he did. He bought her one glass of wine. Tom wasn't sure just how much Celine had had to drink before she found him, but the one glass seemed to hit her pretty hard. She'd started talking about Peter Wilbourne again, Peter Wilbourne and the secret society.

Tom opened his eyes. Celine wouldn't tell him who the leader was, but he knew that she had a strong hunch. She must have been snoop-ing through Elizabeth's things again, because she thought it was hysterically funny that Eliza-beth had thought Peter might be in charge. "He doesn't even know who it is himself!" she'd shrieked. "Mr. Big never talks to the rest of them directly. Sometimes he phones them and sometimes he just leaves them instructions. But he must monitor their meetings somehow, be-cause he always knows what went on."

But Tom, of course, had known that himself. None of the members of the secret society ever saw the leader or heard his voice. When they met with each other, their faces were covered.

"I bet you don't know this," Celine had said, whispering conspiratorially in his ear, "but that society is a national organization. It isn't just here; it's all over. It's tied up with some of the biggest companies in the country."

Tom had known that, too, but he didn't let on to Celine.

"And to show you how stupid Peter is," she'd gone on, "he told me that, about it being this enormous network and how he was going to be set for life once he graduates college, and he still hasn't figured out who the leader is."

Tom's fingers drummed on the arms of his chair. "Then I guess I'm pretty stupid, too," he said aloud. "Because I knew all that and I haven't figured out who it is either."

Tom closed his eyes again, trying to picture every expression on Celine's face, every movement she made while they were talking about the secret society. She must have inadvertently given him some hint of whom she suspected. If only he could remember . . .

When he opened his eyes again, Elizabeth was standing beside him, watching him curiously.

"Elizabeth!" He rubbed his eyes. He must have dozed off for a couple of minutes. "What are you doing here?"

"I thought I'd pick you up a little ear-

cause there's something I have to tell you before we go."

Pick him up early? Before we go? He stared back at her, barely concealing his bewilderment. Or maybe not concealing it at all.

"Don't tell me you forgot!" She put her hands on her hips. "You did forget, didn't you, Tom? You have no idea what I'm talking about."

"Of course I know what you're talking about," he lied, his mind racing backward and forward trying to remember. It was Friday night. He had a vague, pre-night-out-with-Celine memory of Elizabeth asking him to go somewhere with her on Friday night. Actually, it hadn't been an invitation so much as a challenge. Tom grinned in triumph. "Your sister's," he said. "We're going to dinner with your sister and her boyfriend."

Elizabeth was still eyeing him skeptically, but she decided to let it pass. "That's what I wanted to talk to you about," she said, suddenly edgy. "This is a secret you're not allowed to tell anybody, but you have to know before we get there."

He nodded, wondering what she could possibly be getting at. "My lips are sealed."

Elizabeth took a deep breath. "Mike isn't Jessica's boyfriend," she said, rushing her words. "He's her husband."

"Her husband? Jessica and Mike are *married*?"

147

She straightened her bag over her shoulder. "That's right," she said unenthusiastically.

"Well, that's great," Tom said.

Elizabeth glared at him. "It is not," she said flatly. "It's like she's married to the mob."

"Oh, come on, Elizabeth." He got to his feet. "Mike's not that bad."

"He's worse," Elizabeth snapped, leading the way to the door. "You may not believe he's involved with the secret society, but other people do. People who are just as smart and clever as you are."

He switched off the light and followed her. "And who would these smart and clever people be?" he asked, unable to keep the mockery out of his voice. "Not William White, by any chance?"

She stopped in the doorway and faced him. "As a matter of fact, William does agree with me. He thinks there isn't any doubt that Mike's involved."

Tom couldn't keep the sneer out of his voice either. "And when did he tell you all this, at the Thursday-night poetry reading?"

"We didn't go last night," she answered coolly. "William was busy. We talked about it the other day."

Tom locked the door to the station. "I'm surprised you didn't invite William to go with you tonight," he commented. "Since you spend so much time talking to him."

"I would have," she said as she stomped ahead. "But unlike you, he doesn't care for Mike McAllery."

"I knew I was right about Mike," Tom mumbled under his breath. "He must be a great guy."

"This is really delicious," Elizabeth said, holding out her plate to Jessica for another enchilada. Maybe Winston was right about stress. As soon as Elizabeth sat down in the living room and caught a whiff of the smells coming from the kitchen she'd felt famished. "When did you learn to cook like this?" she asked as Jessica spooned extra hot sauce onto Elizabeth's plate. Knowing her twin, she'd been half-expecting peanut-butter sandwiches.

Jessica smiled enigmatically. "Mike's been teaching me to cook," she said, beaming in Mike's direction. "He knows all the secrets."

Hearing his name, Mike looked up for a second and smiled back at Jessica, but then he returned to the intense conversation he was having with Tom about twelve-string guitars. Mike and Tom, it turned out, shared a passion for blues. Tom couldn't get over Mike's incredible record collection, and Mike couldn't get over the extent of Tom's knowledge of the history and development of blues. Neither of them had shut up for more than two minutes since Elizabeth and Tom arrived.

Jessica, sitting beside her, leaned close. "Well?" she whispered. "What do you think?"

Elizabeth took a sip of the beer she was sharing with her twin. As much as she hated to admit it, she wasn't having as bad a time as she'd planned on having. To her surprise, Mike was a perfect host, solicitous and considerate. She'd expected him to be silent and hostile, but instead he was not only talkative but pretty interesting as well. *It must be from hanging out in bars,* Elizabeth reassured herself. *He's had a lot of practice talking to strangers.*

"I think it's a great meal," Elizabeth whispered back. "I'm really proud of you."

Jessica beamed. The last time Elizabeth had seen her sister here, Jessica hadn't been looking her best, but tonight she looked beautiful, as if she'd just stepped out of a fashion magazine. *I guess married life really agrees with her when she isn't lying on the floor crying her heart out,* Elizabeth commented silently.

"And what about the apartment?" Jessica asked. "Don't you love it?"

"It's great," Elizabeth agreed. "It's really cool." The apartment looked a lot better when Mike hadn't just torn it apart. In fact, it was actually very attractive, stylish but warm and unique. One of Mike's other girlfriends must have decorated it for him.

Jessica pressed a little closer. "And what

about Mike?" she asked. "What do you think of him?"

Elizabeth quickly took another mouthful of enchilada. How could Jessica ask her what she thought of Mike when she already knew what Elizabeth thought of Mike? Elizabeth thought he was the scum of the earth.

Rich male laughter sounded from the other side of the table.

"He's being very nice," she admitted grudgingly. He probably knew that Elizabeth had heard about his violent temper and was on his best behavior.

"He really likes Tom." Jessica passed her a bowl of pickled jalapeño peppers, giving her a meaningful look at the same time. "I like him, too," she said. "He's so nice, not to mention attractive."

Elizabeth knew that her sister wasn't making a statement; she was asking a question. Jessica wanted to know if Elizabeth liked Tom. *Really* liked Tom, as Winston would say.

A year or two ago, Elizabeth might have dragged Jessica into the kitchen to ask her if she thought Tom liked Elizabeth. But that was before Jessica married a violent criminal, and before Elizabeth started finding it so difficult to determine how *she* felt about anything.

When she saw Tom like this, acting as though Mike McAllery were the best friend he'd ever had, she wasn't sure if she cared whether or not he liked her. She passed the peppers across to Tom. "He's a terrific investigative reporter," she said simply.

Jessica smiled. "I know what you mean," she said. "Mike's a fantastic mechanic."

Chapter Seven

Jessica woke to find a gentle sunshine spreading over the bed and Mike standing over her with a loaded tray in his hands.

"What's that?" she asked, smiling sleepily.

"Breakfast," he replied, setting down the tray and carefully climbing in beside her. "I figured we deserved a nice long morning after our first successful evening of entertaining." He leaned over and kissed her gently. "Mrs. McAllery," he whispered, "you definitely proved you're the most charming, poised, delightful, and beautiful wife I've ever had." He kissed her again. "And your sister's not bad either."

Jessica snuggled against him. "I told you you'd like Elizabeth. She can be a little serious sometimes, and she isn't as attractive as I am, of course, but she's pretty wonderful."

Mike poured out two cups of coffee. "So

what do you think she thought of us?" he asked. "Do you think she'll go back and give your parents a glowing report?"

If Elizabeth weren't sworn to secrecy, she might. Well, not glowing, maybe, Jessica decided, but not too awful either. Jessica could tell that Elizabeth hadn't had the rotten time she'd expected to have. At least she'd be able to tell their parents that Jessica's life was more normal than she'd thought it would be.

"I'm sure of it. She never stopped talking about how good the enchiladas were and how nice the apartment looks." She took the cup he was handing her. "I think she must've thought you kept your bike in the bedroom or something."

Mike laughed. "I don't know how I got this reputation for being mad, bad, and dangerous to know," he said, "but I hope your sister will tell everyone they're wrong." He gave her a plate with an omelette and home fries. "I'm a really nice guy."

When Jessica didn't say anything, he pretended to pout. "That was your cue, Jess. You're supposed to say, 'Yes, Mike, you're a really nice guy.'"

She popped a slice of potato into his mouth. "I don't want you to get any more vain than you already are."

"No, seriously, baby. Do you think Elizabeth thinks I'm a nice guy?"

Jessica looked into his face. As old, and streetwise, and hard as he could be sometimes, he reminded her of a little boy. He was so earnest and eager to have her sister's good opinion that Jessica felt a sudden jolt of anger toward Elizabeth for not giving it.

"Of course she does," she assured him. "Elizabeth thinks you're terrific."

"Really? How do you know that? What did she say?"

Laughing, she elbowed him away. "You're just like a kid, you know that?"

"Come on, baby," he wheedled. "What did she say?"

She couldn't tell him the truth, that the comment Elizabeth had made when they were in the kitchen together, making coffee, was "He's almost human when he's not throwing you around."

"She said you were one of the most intelligent and attractive men she'd ever met."

"Really?"

Jessica nodded. "She said she'd been a little worried about you before, because of the stories she'd heard, but now that she'd met you, she was really happy for us. She thinks we make a great couple."

Happy as a cat in the sun, he picked up his knife and fork. "We do make a terrific couple. We were made for each other." He started to

155

eat. "And Elizabeth and Tom make a great couple, too. Why does she hang around with that dragonian William White when it's obvious she and Tom are crazy about each other?"

"I'm not so sure it's obvious to them," Jessica answered. "It looks to me like they're going to be the last to know."

Todd finished his last set of push-ups and grabbed a towel from the handlebar of the exercise bike. "So that's about how things stand," he said, wiping the sweat from his face. "The administration doesn't want to take any responsibility for the fact that officially or unofficially, they allowed the sports department to use gifts and privileges to lure the best athletes here and keep them here. They want someone to take the rap for them, and it looks pretty certain that two of those someones are Mark and me."

Winston shook his head. "What a serious drag," he grunted, slowly lowering the weights to the ground. "Why don't you talk to Elizabeth? She and Tom Watts might be able to look into it for you. You know, do a story on how the administration's letting its students take the blame for its mistakes."

Winston had always been able to make Todd laugh, but never more than now. "You must still be suffering the effects of that Sigma hazing," Todd gasped when he had stopped laughing enough to speak. "You don't seriously believe that Elizabeth would do *me* a favor, do you? The only article she'd be interested in writing on me would be my obituary."

Winston took his towel from a Nautilus machine. "I know I'm prejudiced in Elizabeth's favor since she saved my life, Todd, but I really don't believe that's true. Elizabeth isn't a vindictive kind of person."

Todd threw his own towel over Winston's head. "If she's not vindictive, why am I in this mess?" he wanted to know. "Do you think it was a coincidence that she decided to dig up this scandal on the jocks just when we broke up?"

Winston threw the towel back. "Yes," he said unhesitatingly. "I do. And I think you know deep down that I'm right. Why don't you just talk to her? What harm could it do?"

Todd thought of Lauren. Every time he tried to talk to Lauren, they ended up fighting. Winston might not blame Elizabeth, but Lauren did. She didn't seem to care that Todd might lose his scholarship, or his place on the team, or even be asked to leave SVU altogether. All Lauren cared about was that Todd should be angry with Elizabeth for what she'd done.

"Have you ever tried to talk to a woman?" Todd asked as they started toward the showers.

Winston groaned. "Elizabeth thinks I should talk to Denise," he said suddenly, changing the subject so abruptly that Todd stopped in the middle of the hall.

"Elizabeth thinks you should talk to Denise about what?" he asked. "About me?"

Winston shook his head. "No, not about you. About Denise and me. I can't tell if Denise really likes me or not—you know, *really*—and Elizabeth says what I should do is just ask her right out how she feels."

Todd snapped his fingers. "Just like that?"

"Uh-huh," Winston said, pushing open the door to the showers. "Just like that."

"It could work," Todd said, though it sounded a little risky to him. What if Winston asked her how she felt and she told him she felt nothing? The poor guy might never recover. "On the other hand, you could just ask her out and see how she responds to that."

"Ask her out?" Winston was staring at him as though this tried-and-true idea, used by men for centuries, had never occurred to him.

"Yeah." Todd grinned. "Ask her out. Ask her to the charity ball. Even if she turns you down because she's going with someone else, you should be able to tell where you stand with her."

"Ask her out?" Winston repeated. "You mean, just ask her to go to the dance with me?"

"It usually works," Todd said. "If she starts gagging, it means you're the last guy she'd want to go anywhere with. And if she says yes, she either really wants to go to the ball or she really likes you."

Winston sat down on a bench to take off his shoes. "Just ask her out," he muttered to himself. "Now why didn't Elizabeth think of that?"

As people went, Celine Boudreaux was a major pain in the neck in almost every way imaginable. She was bossy, she was dishonest and untrustworthy, she was manipulative and self-centered, she was sloppy, noisy, discourteous, and disrespectful of other people's property and space—and she had a wild streak in her that made the Mississippi during flood season look tame. But even Elizabeth had to admit that there was one advantage to having Celine as your roommate: she could sleep through Marine maneuvers.

Elizabeth was especially grateful for that—Celine's only positive trait—this morning. She'd woken early after a fitful sleep, in which she'd dreamed of Tom, Mike, and Jessica all going off together on Mike's motorcycle, determined to get some real proof that Mike McAllery was behind the secret society, no matter what Tom might say.

So far, though, Elizabeth hadn't managed to do much more than type a few notes onto her computer. *Secret Society,* she'd written, and then under it the names *Mike McAllery* and *Peter*

159

Wilbourne. She'd left a space next to Mike's name with a question mark beside it. If only she could figure out who the second leader might be. *Mike and* who? she wordlessly asked the screen. Who had the right connections, the right sort of mind, and still would be able to work with Mike?

An image from the night before flashed before her eyes. She and Jessica were finishing off the salad, while across from them Mike and Tom were talking excitedly about bottleneck guitars or something like that. The meal hadn't been officially over when they both jumped up from the table and raced into the living room because Mike had a Willie McTell tape that Tom had never heard. Not only that, but Tom had turned out to be a lot more interested in motorcycles than he'd ever let on to Elizabeth. All the two of them did over coffee was yap on about exhausts and cylinders and acceleration.

Tom? It couldn't possibly be. Tom Watts was mysterious, he was enigmatic, he was downright difficult most of the time, but he couldn't be tied in with the secret society. It just couldn't be.

Elizabeth scowled in concentration. What had Isabella said that time about Tom having so many secrets? And William; wasn't William always making little remarks that suggested Tom might not be exactly as he seemed?

She closed her eyes, trying to clear her head,

but all she could see were Mike and Tom on the floor of Mike's living room, going through Mike's CD collection like a couple of kids trading marbles. Did the two of them know each other better than Tom had led her to believe?

The computer hummed softly, but the buzzing in Elizabeth's brain blotted it out. What about William? For no apparent reason, Mike McAllery and Tom Watts disliked William White intensely and didn't care who knew it—even the woman William White was going out with. Last night William's name had come up in passing. "Let's talk about something else," Mike had growled, and Tom, slightly more diplomatic, had immediately changed the subject back to music.

It can't be, it just can't be, a soft but insistent voice was saying in her heart.

But the voice in Elizabeth's heart was being shouted down by her brain. What about the way Tom had tried to discourage her from pursuing the secret society story? He'd shown her those threatening notes, but she had only his word for it that they'd been left to scare him and her off. She'd never gotten any threats herself. Wasn't it strange that Elizabeth, who had openly gone on researching the story, had never been warned off but that Tom, who refused to do anything, had?

And what about—

"What are you doing there, Little Miss Girl Reporter? Meditating?"

And what about Celine? Startled, Elizabeth opened her eyes. Celine was leaning over her shoulder, reading the words on the screen.

"Get out of here, Celine," Elizabeth ordered. "This is none of your business."

"Mike McAllery?" Celine started doing her whooping-crane impersonation, which was supposed to pass for laughter. "Sugar, have you been cleaning your teeth too much or something? Are you seriously suggesting that Mike McAllery is connected with the secret society?"

Elizabeth hit the exit key.

"Why, I may just die laughing," Celine hooted, scattering ash all over Elizabeth's bed as she threw herself across it. "Now I have heard everything."

Elizabeth snapped off the computer and got to her feet. "I'm going to the library to work in peace," she said coldly.

Celine was still laughing as Elizabeth slammed the door shut behind her.

So there were two people who didn't think Mike McAllery could possibly be connected with the society. Elizabeth marched up the path from Dickenson Hall, her notebook pressed against her chest. Wasn't it interesting that those two people were Tom and Celine?

*　　*　　*

Winston took a deep breath. "Denise," he said, calm and suave, like a man accustomed to asking beautiful women out. "Denise, I was wondering if you're not busy, if you'd like to go to the charity ball with me."

No, you gutless dope. He groaned inwardly. *She won't know you're asking her on a real date; she'll think you just want a buddy.*

He stared at his reflection for a second, listening to the words echo through his mind.

He took another deep breath and tried again.

"Denise," Winston said, "why don't we go to the charity ball together?" That sounded a little too cut-and-dried. The only answer she could give to an offer like that was yes or no. He wanted to give her some leeway, so if she didn't want to go out with him, she could at least let him down gently.

Staring hard at himself, he gave it another try. "If you're not busy the night of the charity ball, maybe you'd like to go with—" He broke off. Was that a long nostril hair he saw or something on the mirror? He blew at the glass. It was something on the mirror.

"Once again from the top," Winston said, pulling himself up to his full height and gazing levelly at his own eyes. "Denise, do you have a date for the charity ball?"

He thought about it for a second. That was good. In one simple sentence he was establishing that what he was doing was asking her for a date, not offering to keep her company because no one else had. If she did already have a date, she could then say something along the lines of, "Yes, Winnie, I'm going with Tom Cruise." If she didn't have a date, she could say no and when he asked her to go with him, she would know what he meant and have time to think of some way of getting out of it without actually demolishing his feelings.

Winston rubbed his hands together. He was beginning to get the hang of this; it wasn't as bad as he'd thought. He closed his eyes and pretended that he had asked Denise if she had a date for the ball and that she had said Tom Cruise was busy that night so she was staying in. "Well, what about going with me?" he asked.

He opened his eyes. That sounded pathetic, really pathetic. That wasn't confident and masculine. That wasn't Tarzan reaching out and yanking Jane down from the tree. It was weak and sniveling. *What about going with* me? "What about it?" she was likely to snap back.

"Let's get a grip on ourself," Winston advised his reflection. "Let's try the bolder approach."

He cleared his throat. "Denise," he boomed. "You want to go to the charity dance with me or what?"

Too crude. It wasn't so much the bold approach as the route of the Neanderthal.

"Denise, I'd be really proud, not to say delighted, not to say berserk with joy, if you'd agree to go to the charity ball with me."

Winston groaned. He sounded like a moron, that's what he sounded like. A big, stupid moron. She'd probably be asleep before he got past the word *joy*.

Why was he having so much trouble with this? He'd asked girls out before. He'd asked tons of girls out before. But the truth was that he didn't enjoy it. He didn't know any man who did, except maybe someone like Bruce Patman, who had an ego bigger than Mount Rushmore. Asking a girl out was like running into oncoming traffic: there was a chance the traffic might stop in time, but on the whole you were begging to be run down.

Besides, Denise wasn't just a girl. She was special. A goddess among women. A diamond among marbles.

Someone rapped sharply on the door. "Winnie? Are you in there?"

Denise!

If it weren't attached, Winston might have swallowed his tongue. "Ya—here!" he cried, but it was a strangled cry by anybody's standards.

The door opened and the dream-inspiring head of Denise Waters peeked in. "You talking to yourself again, Winnie?" she asked with a

165

grin. "At least you know you'll never be lonely."

But I am lonely! he wanted to shout back. *I am lonely, Denise. Lonely for you!* Instead he gurgled.

She narrowed her eyes. "Are you okay? You look a little funny."

"I'm okay," he managed to squeak. "I—I'm fine. I'm okay."

"Why do you sound so weird?"

"Do I?" he squeaked. "I don't think I sound weird."

She grinned some more. "Well, you wouldn't, would you?"

His palms were beginning to sweat. He hadn't even started and already his palms were sweating. He had to get her out of here. He needed to practice some more; he wasn't ready.

"Denise," Winston said, this time sounding almost normal. "Was there something you wanted? I'm kind of busy at the moment."

Denise nodded. "Yeah," she said. "I wanted to know if you want to go to the charity ball with me."

He didn't trust himself to speak.

"You don't have a date already, do you?"

Winston shook his head.

"So what do you say? Do you want to go?"

"Umph," Winston gasped.

"You can say no if you want."

"N-no. Yes, I mean, yes. That'd be great."

"Cool," Denise said. "See you later, Winnie." And she shut the door.

Winston turned back to the mirror. "You see," he told the smiling young man in the glass. "I told you it was going to be easy."

"I don't get you, man!" Tom was trying not to shout, but it wasn't working. Several passersby turned to look at him. "All semester you've tried to drag me out with you every opportunity you get, and now when I'm asking—begging—you to double with me for the charity ball, you refuse."

Danny fixed him with a look that might have been disappointed or might have been simply exasperated. "Tombo," he said, not shouting at all. "I tried to get you out for your own good. You work too hard. You don't have any fun. I'm your best friend, Tom; I love you like a brother. I only had your best interests at heart. Every pizza I invited you to share, every movie I asked you to come to, every party you didn't want to know about . . . All that was for you, Tom, so you could have some fun."

Tom was beginning to think that God didn't like him. First he had Celine driving him nuts, and now Danny.

"Then why won't you double with me for the charity ball?" He was still shouting. "I would've thought you and Izzy would be happy to go with me."

Danny turned left. "We would be happy to go with you, Tom. You know we would. Isabella and I are two of your biggest fans. If you were taking Elizabeth Wakefield to the dance, we'd be right there beside you." He stopped at the entrance to the gym. "But you're not going by yourself, Tom, and you're not going with Elizabeth. You're going with the most lethal thing to come out of the South since moonshine."

"So what?" Tom followed Danny through the doors. "You don't have to dance with her. Isabella doesn't have to dance with her. I'm the one who's stuck with her all evening."

Danny looked over his shoulder. "You mean you're the one who asked her to go."

Tom was tempted to tell Danny the truth: that he didn't actually remember inviting Celine to the dance, but Celine remembered, which was more or less the same thing. In fact, Tom was pretty sure that he hadn't invited Celine, but she called him after the night Peter Wilbourne stood her up and thanked him for seeing her safely home. She said she hoped she hadn't been too tipsy, but she hadn't had any supper that night and the wine had gone straight to her head. She said she was absolutely thrilled that he'd asked her to the charity ball and she was looking forward to it.

Tom had to give her one thing—she was clever. She knew he wouldn't deny inviting her, because she knew she'd said too much about the secret society.

"What's the big deal?" Tom roared as Danny charged down the steps to the locker room. "We go to the ball together. We drink a little punch together. We go home. It's only a couple of hours, Danny; surely you could spare a couple of hours for your best friend."

Danny stopped suddenly, leaning against the railing. "I could," he admitted. "I could do it for you, Tom, and under most circumstances, I would. But Izzy won't. If I tell her that we're doubling with you and Celine, she'll tell me to go to the ball by myself."

Tom had to resist the temptation to say, *So?*

He sighed wearily. He was going to be trapped with Celine for the whole night, cast off in a corner because no one he liked liked Celine, listening to her criticize everyone else's dates and clothes and trying to avoid her octopuslike arms that were always twisting themselves around him.

Tom scowled. The things he did for Elizabeth Wakefield. If she only knew.

"You won't even talk to me at the ball?" he asked calmly. "You won't even come over and say hello?"

Danny shook his head. "You know, Tom, no matter how long I know you, I will probably never understand you."

"Is that a 'yes I will talk to you' or a 'no I won't?' "

"Just answer me one question," Danny persisted. "One simple question."

Another weary sigh shuddered through Tom's body. He had the feeling he already knew what that question was.

"Shoot."

Danny put a hand on his shoulder. "What are you doing, Tombo? You know you don't like Celine. I know you don't like Celine. Probably even Celine knows you don't like Celine, only she wouldn't care. Why are you going out with her?"

Like a trusty dog hurrying to save its master in the storm, an old line came to Tom that he used when he was Wildcat Watts, the man with a different date every night.

Tom smiled the sly, self-confident smile he used to smile. "She's got nice legs."

Maybe married life isn't so bad after all, Jessica was thinking as the lowrider cut sharply around a bend and she pressed closer to Mike. *This sure beats sitting in the dorm studying.*

Jessica smiled into Mike's back. She was feeling happy, really happy, for the first time in weeks. Mike had been in a terrific mood all day. Not only had he fixed her breakfast in bed, kissed her till she was breathless, given her a backrub, and finally promised to take her to the charity ball, but he'd decided to knock off work for the day and take her for a ride on the bike and a romantic picnic in a secluded cove he knew of. For a change, Jessica didn't wonder how he'd found the cove, or what woman he'd taken there before. She'd just relaxed and enjoyed herself.

Now, as they turned toward their apartment building, she started to make plans for the night. Maybe a candlelight dinner, a little wine, a video . . .

Jessica was still trying to decide what kind of movie she'd like to see as they rode into the parking lot and Mike cut the engine.

"It's good to be back home," he said, sliding off the bike and lifting her into his arms. "I can't wait to get you upstairs, Mrs. McAllery. This has been one of the best days of my life, and I want to show you my appreciation."

Too happy to remember that Steven Wakefield, Zorro of SVU, might be standing at his window watching them, Jessica slipped her arms around Mike's neck and lost herself in a passionate kiss.

"I love you, baby," Mike whispered, his mouth moving along her face and down her neck. "I love you so."

"Isn't this cozy."

Steven hadn't been standing at his window;

he'd been standing in the entrance to the building.

At the sound of her brother's voice Jessica pulled out of Mike's embrace. But Steven wasn't talking to her. He was talking to Mike.

"So how was your little dinner party?" Steven asked. "It looks like you must have had a pretty good time."

Mike took a step forward. "Look, Steve," he said, one hand raised as if gesturing for a truce. "I don't want to keep fighting with you over nothing."

"Nothing?" Steven laughed. "You call my sister nothing? You call dragging my sister into your sleazy world *nothing*?"

Mike took another step forward. "Will you stop acting like some damn caveman?" he demanded. "I don't see why you have to jump on me every time you see me. Why can't we just let it go? If you don't want to be friendly, that's fine, but I'm getting really tired of this. I didn't do anything to deserve it."

"Oh, no?" This time it was Steven who stepped forward. "You think my sister was living with guys in high school, Motorcycle Man? My sister was innocent until she met you." He shoved Mike so hard, Mike almost lost his balance.

"Steven!" Jessica screamed. "Steven, please!"

Mike stepped in front of her, knocking Steven back. "And you can stop calling her your

172

sister!" he shouted. "Because she isn't your sister, she's my wife."

Jessica felt the air leave her body. In the silent second after Mike's announcement all she could hear was the blood rushing through her.

And then all she heard was Steven Wakefield's fist smacking against Mike McAllery's face. "You liar!" Steven shouted. "You rotten liar. Don't ever let me hear you say anything like that again."

Mike picked himself off the ground. "You mean you didn't tell him?" he asked Jessica. "You didn't tell him you're my wife?"

"Don't let him bully you, Jessica," Steven ordered. "Don't let him intimidate you."

Jessica couldn't move. The words were out in the air now: final, forever, flapping frantically toward Calico Drive and Ned and Alice Wakefield. Now she really was married. Married forever.

"Tell him I'm not lying, baby," Mike was saying, his eyes hanging on to her like claws. "Jess, tell Steven you're my wife."

"You really are something, aren't you?" Steven sneered. "You just never give up."

"Jessica!" Mike's voice was like a knife cutting through the early evening. "Jessica, tell him! Tell him you're my wife!"

But Jessica was already running down the street, running fast so that she wouldn't have to see the tears in Mike's eyes.

Chapter Eight

Jessica opened her eyes. Although a sword of sunlight was cutting through the crack in the curtains, the room was still dark and full of shadowy shapes. Exhausted from bad dreams and another night of sobbing herself to sleep, Jessica didn't know where she was. Every part of her felt numb: her mind, her body—even her heart.

She propped herself up on one elbow and looked around, trying to make out something familiar. *Maybe I had an accident and I have amnesia,* she told herself. *Maybe this really is my room, but I can't remember.* Someone turned on a radio in the next room. "Mike!" Jessica breathed. She didn't have amnesia. She knew exactly who she was. She was Mrs. Michael McAllery, and Mike was outside, waiting for her.

The numbness vanished instantly, replaced by a panic close to terror as the events of the night before came rushing back. Mike and Steven pushing each other around in the parking lot. Mike shouting, "Tell him you're my wife!" Jessica herself running away, running and running until she couldn't see through her tears or run anymore.

Jessica sat up, clutching the blankets to her chest, trying to calm herself down as she stared at the door, waiting for it to burst open and Mike to come shouting into the room, kicking and throwing everything out of his way until he got to her.

"It's all right," Jessica told herself above the heavy pounding of her heart. "This isn't Mike's room . . . This isn't Mike's bed . . ." She looked at the poster taped to the back of the door. "This is Izzy's room!"

Jessica fell back on the pillows, tears of relief filling her eyes. How could she have forgotten? After she fled the scene in the parking lot, she got on the first bus she saw and came here, to the room she used to share with Isabella, praying all the way that Isabella would be home alone. *Please*, she'd begged as the bus neared the campus. *Please don't let her be out. Please don't let Danny be there.* Miraculously, Isabella had been home—and had been alone. Isabella hadn't even seemed surprised to find her old roommate standing on her doorstep in a hurricane of tears.

"Come on in, Jess," she'd said, putting an arm around her. "I was just making some tea."

Jessica had never been so glad to see anyone before in her life. Supportive and understanding as ever, Isabella had asked no questions but listened as Jessica poured out her story over the course of the long, teary evening.

There was a gentle rapping at the door, but even though Jessica knew it couldn't be Mike, she jumped. "Yes?" Her voice was hoarse from crying.

Isabella peeped in. "Just checking to see if you were awake yet." She opened the door a little farther so that light fell across Jessica's bed. "How are you doing?" she asked gently. "You get any sleep?"

Jessica nodded. "A little, but you couldn't call it quality time."

Isabella came over and sat on the edge of the bed. "Why don't you stay here for a few days, Jess, till things settle down and you can get yourself together a little?"

An image of what number 2C, Mimosa Apartments, probably looked like right at this instant appeared in Jessica's mind. It probably looked like a battlefield, with furniture kicked over and things pulled off the shelves. He might even have thrown all her things out the window. It was something Mike was more than capable of.

"Are you sure it's all right?"

"Am I sure it's all right?" Isabella gave her a shake. "Hey, you can move back in here permanently, Jess, anytime you want. All you have to do is say the word."

Jessica made no comment. She'd given Isabella a slightly edited version of what had happened last night, carefully omitting any mention of the fact that she and Mike were husband and wife.

Isabella got to her feet. "I promised Danny I'd study with him today, so I have to run, but there's a pot of coffee made and there's plenty of food in the fridge." She brushed a strand of golden hair from Jessica's face. "My advice to you is to stay in all day. Forget about everything, even midterms. Just try to relax a little and straighten out your head."

Jessica nodded. "You're right, Izzy. That's exactly what I'll do."

Isabella's expression became stern. "And *don't* call him, Jess. Whatever you do, don't call him. You and Mike need to put a little space between you."

"You're right." Jessica nodded again. "I'm not going to talk to him for a couple of days. I'm going to straighten out my head and then decide what to do."

"Good girl." Isabella smiled. "I'll bring a pizza back with me tonight and we can do some more studying. How does that sound?"

No fighting, no screaming, no arguing just to have a little time to herself to do what she wanted. Just pizza and history and easy companionship. Jessica smiled back. "That sounds great."

"So I guess it wasn't as bad as you thought it would be," Nina prodded, not very gently.

Elizabeth made a grudging face. "He didn't throw the dinner out the window, if that's what you mean."

Celine didn't get up till well past noon on Sundays, so Elizabeth and Nina were studying for their English exam in Nina's room. Elizabeth had hoped it would get her mind off Mike and Tom for at least a little while.

Elizabeth should have known better. Nina had wanted every single detail of the dinner at the McAllerys, and for Elizabeth every detail was like a nail in her heart. *Mike and Tom, Mike and Tom,* she kept thinking. Her mind told her it had to be true, but her heart stubbornly insisted that it couldn't be.

Nina gave her a tolerant smile. "Come on, Elizabeth," she coaxed. "Admit it. It sounds to me like Mike and Jessica are really happy together. You thought it was going to be all squalor and fighting and motorcycle parts on the dining-room table, and instead it was just a regular evening with a nice couple."

A nice couple of thugs, Elizabeth thought, her mind instantly back to Mike and Tom, the place where it seemed to want to stay.

"It doesn't mean I have to like him," Elizabeth argued. "Maybe he isn't a bad host, but that doesn't mean I have to make the creep my friend." Not the way she'd made that other creep, Tom Watts, her friend.

Nina wasn't listening to her. "It just goes to show, doesn't it?" she continued, her smile almost dreamy. "You really never can tell, can you?"

"You sure can't," Elizabeth agreed wholeheartedly. The nicest, most intelligent person you'd ever known could turn out to be a fascist in disguise.

Nina picked up an apple from the bowl on the floor between them. "Are Jessica and Mike going to be at the charity ball?" she asked. "Are we all going to trade a couple of dances? William won't have to sit up front the whole time, will he?"

Elizabeth's throat tightened. She couldn't very well tell Nina that her brother-in-law, mastermind of the attack on her and Bryan, wouldn't want to dance with her. Nor could she tell Nina that she and Bryan weren't exactly William's favorite people either. She was tempted to get a bad headache that night and stay home.

"I think Jess and Mike mentioned something about the ball," Elizabeth mumbled vaguely. In fact, Jessica had brought it up, somehow assuming that Elizabeth and Tom were going together and that the four of them could double. The mistake had been so embarrassing to both Elizabeth and Tom that he had knocked over his water glass and Elizabeth had choked on a tortilla chip. "I guess we'll just have to see what happens."

Steven broke a croissant in half and spread it with butter and jelly. "I shouldn't have let him get away with it, Billie," he was saying to the spot where he assumed her head must be. A fuzzy photograph of some politician smiled back at him. "I know I have my future law career to think of, but I should've fought harder. I pulled back because I was worried about what my father would say if he found out I was brawling in a parking lot, but I should have knocked his teeth out when I had the chance."

From behind the Sunday paper, Billie grunted. "Sure, you should have."

"You don't believe me, do you?" Steven demanded, licking a blob of jelly from his hand. "You think I'm afraid of Mike McAllery just because he's tough."

"I think you're losing your mind," Billie said evenly, staying well behind the newspaper.

Steven shook his croissant in the air. "I could have taken him, Billie. He's not as tough as he looks, you know."

"He gave you a black eye, Steven. What did you want, two?"

"That was later," Steven protested. After Jessica ran off, Mike suddenly pulled back and hit him so hard he actually saw stars. Then he stepped over Steven's prone body, started up his bike, and tore off in the opposite direction from Jessica. "I shoved him halfway across the parking lot before he reacted at all."

"Maybe he was trying not to embarrass you in front of your sister," Billie said. "Or maybe he was thinking of Jess. Maybe he has a rule about beating the stuffing out of his girlfriend's brother."

His laugh was as hollow as a drum. "Oh, sure, Billie, he was thinking of Jess. That's why he tried to wind me up by telling me they were married. That's why he sent her running off in tears."

The newspaper was slowly lowered. Billie sighed. "Steven," she said, "you have been ranting on about your scene with Mike last night since it happened. I've heard every detail of it so many times that I can't believe I wasn't there with you. I can see Mike and Jess pull into the parking lot. I can see them kissing. I can see Mike McAllery taunting you. You've told me all

182

the things you should have done and all the things you should have said, but there's one tiny little thing you seem to have overlooked."

Steven stared back at her. There was nothing he'd overlooked. Even after the pain in his eye subsided, he'd lain awake, replaying every second of their encounter in his mind. He shouldn't have let Mike get away with hitting him.

"And would the attorney for the defense like to tell me what she thinks that one tiny little thing is?" he asked sarcastically.

"Sure." Billie leaned toward him, her expression wry but concerned. "Maybe they really are married, Steven. Have you thought of that?"

Steven stared back at her, at a rare loss for words. Married? Was it really possible that Mike had been telling the truth—that his little sister was Mike McAllery's wife?

"That's impossible," Steven blustered, trying to forget the look of anguish in Mike McAllery's face as he was shouting for Jessica to say they were married. "Even Jessica's not that stupid."

Billie raised her paper again. "Don't be so sure."

The coffeehouse was so busy in the afternoon that William, tired of waiting for someone to come and take their order, had gone to give it to the kitchen himself.

This is better, Elizabeth told herself as the noise and laughter of the other customers blocked out the clamor of her own thoughts. If only she could decide what to do about Tom. Should she confront him with her suspicions and see how he defended himself? Or should she go to the college authorities with the information she did have and let them handle it?

William, so handsome that several pairs of female eyes followed him as he crossed the café, came back to the table carrying two steaming cups of cappuccino.

"Here you go," he said, setting them down. "This will put a smile back on that beautiful face."

Elizabeth forced the beautiful face to smile. "It's midterms," she said feebly. "I just can't seem to concentrate on anything else."

He tilted his head to one side, looking at her appraisingly. "You sure?" he asked. "When I bumped into you, you didn't look like a woman who was worried about the Cavalier poets. You looked like a woman with real problems."

That's the trouble with dating a sensitive man, Elizabeth thought. *It's hard to fool them.* The truth was that, unable to keep her mind on studying, she'd made an excuse to Nina and gone for a walk to try to get her head straight. That was when she ran into William, striding across the quad like a young lord striding across the manor. He'd realized immediately that something was wrong and swept her off for a cup of coffee.

Elizabeth gazed into those pale, haunting eyes. Sometimes they seemed so cold they almost made her shiver, but at other times, like now, they had an almost hypnotic, calming effect. She chewed on her bottom lip, wondering how much she should say. Despite the fact that she never quite felt comfortable confiding in William, he was the one person she knew who had known Tom in his Wildman Watts days. She'd even come across a photograph in one of the old newspapers of Tom and William together at a university fund-raising dinner.

She turned her attention to slowly stirring her cappuccino. "You used to know Tom when he was a football star, didn't you?" she asked casually.

William ripped the top off a bag of sugar. "Everybody knew Tom then," he said stiffly, not bothering to disguise the fact that he didn't count knowing Tom Watts as a major triumph. "He was the biggest thing on campus except the clock tower."

"I'm just curious," Elizabeth quickly explained. "He's such a hard person to get to know . . . Has he changed a lot since then?"

William shrugged. "Tom and I have never been close," he admitted. He smiled disarmingly. "And you must have noticed that his interest in you hasn't exactly made us best friends."

Elizabeth felt herself blush. At the same time William's admitting that he disliked Tom because of his friendship with Elizabeth made her feel better about William. She couldn't help wondering if William wasn't the person she could confide in after all.

"I was just wondering . . . you know . . ." She carefully laid her spoon at the side of her cup. "I was just wondering if you think that Tom is the kind of person who would . . ." Her voice trailed off. It seemed strange to be sitting here like this talking about sinister organizations and dangerous men.

"Would what?" he pressed. He touched one of her fingertips with one of his, so delicately that if she hadn't been staring at their hands, she might not have noticed. "Would he belong to the secret society? Is that what you want to know, Elizabeth?"

She raised her eyes to his, nodding silently.

William leaned back, tapping on the rim of his saucer with his teaspoon. "I wasn't going to say anything," he began. "That's why I told you I'd never heard of the society when you first brought it up. I was hoping I could discourage you from getting too involved in the story."

Every nerve in her body was tense. "You

mean you were worried about me?"

He looked surprised. "Of course I was worried about you, Elizabeth. I didn't want you getting mixed up with those vigilantes. Especially after what happened to your friend." The spoon clattered to the table as his eyes bored into hers. "Especially when you were working so closely with Tom."

Elizabeth hadn't realized that she was holding her breath until she started breathing again. "So you do think he was a member?" she said softly.

William raised an eyebrow. "*Was* a member?" he asked. "Don't you mean *is* a member?"

Her hand started to tremble, and she couldn't speak. As sure as she'd been that her suspicions were right, having William confirm them made her realize how much she'd wanted to be wrong.

"I tried to warn you." William put his hand over hers. "But I knew if I came right out and said something about Tom, you'd think I was just being jealous."

Still stunned, Elizabeth wrapped her fingers around his. At least there was one man she could trust.

After Isabella left, Jessica got dressed and went into the kitchen for a cup of coffee and something to eat. She had a strong craving for something sweet. A doughnut, maybe, or a cheese Danish. Mike had a sweet tooth, too, and some Sunday mornings he'd go out early for pastries and they'd lie in bed till afternoon, reading the papers and sprinkling crumbs all over the bed.

Jessica peered into Isabella's tiny refrigerator. The only sweet thing in it was a jar of strawberry jam. Strawberry jam was Mike's favorite. Jessica decided she'd have cereal instead.

The morning dragged on and Jessica dragged herself with it, wandering aimlessly from the bedroom to the living room and back again. Once this had been her home, but now she felt oddly out of place. She had nothing to do; nothing here belonged to her. Isabella's books were on the shelves, Isabella's clothes thrown over the backs of chairs, Isabella's food in the refrigerator, Isabella's magazines on the coffee table. She shuffled through the CDs. There was a blues song she really wanted to hear right now, but Isabella didn't have it.

Jessica threw herself onto the sofa, thinking about Mike. As much as he scared her when he lost his temper, she knew that the mess they were in wasn't all his fault. He was childish, he was violent, and he was possessive and demanding, but those weren't really the things that were driving them apart. If she was honest with herself, she knew what was really driving them apart: he wanted more than Jessica had bargained on giving.

"Marriage," Jessica said, staring up at the ceiling. She'd had no idea what marriage was like. If she'd thought about it at all, she'd thought it was like a long date. Instead of a movie and a pizza and a kiss in the car you had lots of movies, lots of pizzas, and lots of kisses. But it wasn't like that. It was more like being in an open prison.

Restless, Jessica took the gold locket from around her neck and held it open in the palm of her hand. Inside was a picture of Mike, taken in a photo booth on a day she'd never forget. They'd taken his bike to one of those seaside towns with a boardwalk and rides and fortune-tellers. He looked like the happiest man in the world.

"I love you," Jessica whispered to the snapshot as new tears filled her eyes. "I really, really love you." Once more she saw him as he'd been yesterday, hurt and confused and furious beyond belief, shouting at her to tell Steven the truth.

Why hadn't she told Steven the truth? Why hadn't she told Steven the truth weeks ago?

Because you don't want to be married, she silently answered herself. *That's why. You want to be in love, but you don't want to be married.*

Her body shook with sobs. "But I want to be with Mike," she argued with herself. "I do. I can't stand being without him. I can't stand hurting him like this . . ."

Maybe she hadn't been trying hard enough; maybe that was all it was. You couldn't expect to turn from a frivolous teenager into a mature married woman overnight, could you? Maybe if she'd been a little more understanding of his feelings, maybe if she'd given just a little bit more, they could have worked things out. She'd wanted to be with Mike and still live life like a single woman. No wonder he resented her friends and her college life. No wonder he was insecure.

Jessica closed her eyes, hot tears coursing down her cheeks, remembering the tears in Mike's eyes yesterday when she'd refused to back him up. How could she expect him not to be jealous, not to be possessive, not to lose his temper when she treated him like that? He'd wanted a wife and all he'd gotten was a girl-friend.

"And not a very good girlfriend either." Jessica sniffled. She wouldn't blame him if he started running around with other women again. She had practically driven him into their waiting arms.

The phone started to ring. If it hadn't been right beside her on the coffee table—and if she hadn't been so upset that she wasn't thinking clearly—Jessica wouldn't have answered. But she pressed the handset to her ear before she knew what she'd done.

"Yes?" she whispered, trying to hide the fact that she was crying.

"Jess?"

Her heart dove toward her stomach. It was Mike.

"Where are you?" she whispered.

"I'm downstairs in a phone booth." His voice sounded tired and strained. "I've come to take you home."

Rather than putting a smile back on her face, Elizabeth's coffee with William had made her more restless and upset than she'd been before. William had offered to drive her back to her dorm, but she'd refused. The only thing that helped when she felt like this was exercise, she told him. If she went for a fast walk, she was sure she'd feel better. "So let's play some tennis," he'd suggested. "I can get a court at a moment's notice." But Elizabeth had wanted to be alone.

Now, as she marched purposefully across the abandoned athletics field, Elizabeth suddenly wished that she'd taken William up on his offer after all. Coming toward her, an expression on his handsome face as gloomy as her own, was Todd Wilkins.

Elizabeth glanced around. She was standing in the middle of the track, with no buildings or trees near for yards and yards. There was nowhere to hide. She realized her heart was pounding.

Just walk right by him, she advised herself. *Smile, and walk right by.*

She almost managed to walk right by him. Todd was so immersed in his own thoughts that he didn't even see her until they'd almost collided.

He jumped back in surprise. "Elizabeth!"

She smiled. "Hi, Todd," she said. She gestured vaguely to the rolling lawn surrounding the track. "I was just taking a walk."

"Me too." He smiled awkwardly. "It helps me unwind."

"Me too." Elizabeth shifted from one foot to the other. "Well," she said, preparing to walk right on by. "I guess I'll see you around."

Almost as though it were against his will, he reached out and grabbed hold of her arm. "Elizabeth," he said, his face pink with embarrassment. "I was wondering if I could talk to you about something."

She knew without having to ask what he wanted to talk about. Todd and his friend Mark Gathers were two of the prime suspects in the sports scandal, and word was out that the administration was planning to come down hard on them.

"Look, Todd, I'm really sorry about what happened. I know you blame me—"

"I don't blame you, Elizabeth," he said,

cutting her off. He managed a crooked smile. "I admit I've had a few moments when I wished you'd never learned to type, but you didn't create the illegal practices; you just reported them."

She must have looked as surprised as she felt, because he started to laugh.

"Okay, I haven't always had that well balanced a view, but in my less self-pitying moments I know that's the truth."

Elizabeth recovered her voice. "Well, I'm glad you feel like that, Todd. I would hate for you to think that I—that I—" She couldn't quite manage the words *tried to get you in trouble because you dumped me for Lauren.*

But she didn't have to.

"Exposed the scandal because you were mad at me?" he asked. He blushed again. "I've had my moments of thinking that, too," he admitted. "But Winston pointed out that you're the last person in the world to do something like that, and I realized he was right."

Elizabeth opened her mouth, but nothing came out.

"Actually," Todd said, "Winston's the reason I'm talking to you now. He thought maybe you could help me."

"Help you?"

Todd nodded. "It looks like the administration's going to use me and Mark as their scapegoats," he

193

explained. "They don't want to come out of this thing looking bad—which is exactly how they'll look if they accept the responsibility for what happened. So they're going to let us take the blame."

"But that's not fair!" Elizabeth protested immediately. This was the last thing she'd imagined happening when she and Tom began the piece. "It's the administration that allowed the privileges and special deals. They can't blame you for that."

"Tell me about it," said Todd. "But not only are we going to be blamed, we might find ourselves out in the cold."

Elizabeth sighed, trying to take this in. Why was it always so easy to find justice in movies and so difficult in real life?

"But what do you want me to do?" she asked. "I have no say with the administration. In fact, they've been down on Tom lately because of the way he runs the TV station. You might be better off getting help from someone else."

Todd shook his head. "There is no one else." The smile left his face, and for the first time she saw the anguish he must be going through. "I don't know where to turn, Elizabeth," he confessed, his voice cracking slightly. "I'm going out of my mind worrying, and the more I say that I'm innocent, the harder even I'm finding it to believe."

"But you are innocent." Elizabeth had told

Todd what she was planning before she started the story, and he'd told her from the start that he hadn't done anything wrong. She'd believed him then, and she believed him now. "I don't see how anyone could doubt that."

He grinned ironically. "Thanks for saying that, Liz."

"Look, Todd," Elizabeth said, finding it difficult to take on another problem at this moment. "I can't promise anything, but I'll think about it, okay? I'll see what I can do to help." She made a wry face. "After all, I did my part to create this; I guess I should do something to fix it."

He grabbed both her hands in his, with so much warmth and enthusiasm that she was transported back to the days when they were the perfect couple, the couple who would last forever.

"Thanks, Elizabeth," he said, his voice deep with emotion. "I knew I could count on you."

By the time Dickenson Hall loomed into sight, Elizabeth was so happy to see it that she didn't even care if Celine was at home or not. Celine might be a noxious pain in the neck, but at least Elizabeth knew where she was with Celine. There weren't any hidden corners or secrets: what you saw was what you got. The fact that it was all bad was almost a relief.

Elizabeth strolled down the hallway, almost looking forward to an evening spent exchanging

195

sarcastic remarks with her roommate. At least it would take her mind off other things. Mike, for instance. Todd, for another instance. She put her hand on the knob and turned.

"Tom!"

He was the last person she was expecting to see, but there he was, sitting stiffly at her desk, a small box on his lap.

"I don't know where Celine is—"

"Shut the door, Elizabeth," Tom said softly. "You and I have to talk."

Elizabeth shut the door, overcome with nervousness and an almost irrational fear. Two hours ago she'd still thought of him as Tom, but after what William had told her, she had begun to think of Tom as *him.*

He's not going to hurt you, she scolded herself. *No matter what, you must know that.* She stared at his dark eyes. How did she know that? There was nothing else she'd thought she knew about him that still seemed to be true; why should she be so sure of that?

"I don't know what you mean," she said, stalling for time to pull herself together. She put down her things and crossed over to the chair beside the desk. "I thought we'd done all the talking we had to do."

"Not quite all of it." Tom's eyes were on the box he was holding, his voice strained but steady. "You and I have been working at cross-purposes

196

for a while now, Elizabeth, and I know you've been disappointed in me. I've been trying to get you to give up on the secret society story, and you've been determined to go ahead with it no matter what." He raised his eyes to hers again. "This isn't easy for me, Elizabeth. I've been struggling with this since the whole thing started . . ." Tom's voice trailed off. He moistened his lips and started again. "Well, I guess I thought you'd be more than disappointed in me if I told you the truth. But that doesn't matter; it's time you knew one of the reasons I've been so opposed to your doing this piece."

Elizabeth sat down, holding on to the arm of the chair for support. Her heart was racing, and ice water was running through her veins. "I think I already know what it is."

Tom opened the box, acting as though he hadn't heard her. "I'm not going to get into my whole personal history," he said. "Let's just say that I used to be different, okay? I used to be a BMOC, really full of myself." There was tissue paper in the box, and he carefully pulled it open. "Then something happened that turned everything upside down for me. I finally woke up and realized that I'd been letting my ego rule my life, that I'd been putting all my energy into the wrong things. So I changed. But before I changed, this was part of my life, just like the football, and the parties, and all the other stuff."

He reached inside and removed a silver ring in the shape of a broken star.

Elizabeth touched it. It was cool and smooth. It made her feel afraid again. "What is it?" she asked, hardly able to get the words out.

Tom dropped the star into her hand. "It's the ring that identifies a member of the secret society."

"So it's true," she breathed, remembering the way William had looked when she asked if he thought Tom belonged. She couldn't take her eyes off the small piece of silver in her palm. "You are one of the leaders."

"One of the leaders?" The genuine bafflement in his voice made her look up. "One of the leaders of what?"

Elizabeth stared back at him, the fear dissolving into confusion. He wasn't acting; he couldn't be.

What was wrong with her now? Her hunch had been right, but instead of feeling pleased with herself and vindicated, she felt more than ever that she'd made some horrible mistake. Here she was, sitting with the broken star in her hand and Tom confessing his involvement in the society, and she still couldn't seem to accept that he was behind all that hatred and violence. Part of her was still refusing to believe it was true.

"Of the society," Elizabeth said in a flat, empty voice.

Tom looked as though he might have

laughed if he hadn't been so totally astounded by her accusation.

"Elizabeth," he said patiently. "I wasn't trying to discourage you from doing the story because I didn't want you to find out I was the leader. If I were the leader, I wouldn't have left threatening notes for *me*, would I? I would have made pretty sure that I scared you off right at the start."

"Then why did you try to discourage me?"

He took the ring out of her hand, holding it up to the light. "Because I know what these people are like, Elizabeth. I didn't want them to hurt you." He glanced back at her. "And because I was afraid you'd find out that I once belonged and you'd lose all respect for me."

She felt like someone had put her brain on a merry-go-round, it was spinning so fast. Whom should she trust? Tom? William? Her own heart?

"And why are you telling me all this now?" she asked softly.

Tom's fingers closed around the ring. "Because everything's gone really quiet all of a sudden, like something's about to happen." He stared at his fist. "I have this feeling that you're getting really close, Elizabeth." He looked at her with eyes full of emotion. "And I don't want you to get there alone."

Chapter
Nine

"I don't get it," Isabella said. "You told me you and Mike were definitely coming to the charity ball."

Jessica bit her lip. Normally, she could go shopping every hour of the day and never meet anyone she knew. It was just her luck to run into Isabella, today of all days. Glancing at the list in her hand, Jessica marched up the aisle of the drugstore, searching for the only brand of shaving cream that Mike would use. "Well, we changed our mind, didn't we?" she said over her shoulder.

"What do you mean, you *changed your mind*?" Isabella demanded. "You were excited about the ball. I even remember exactly what you were going to wear."

Jessica remembered, too. She was going to wear her strapless flamingo-pink gown, matching heels, and tiny diamonds in her ears. She was going to be the most beautiful woman at the dance and make Mike proud.

"Well, now I'm not excited about it," Jessica snapped. "We decided that we'd rather just stay home and watch a video."

"*You?*" hooted Isabella. "*You* want to stay home and watch a video instead of going to one of the major social events of the season?"

Jessica thumped down the next aisle. Of course she didn't want to stay home in her jeans and sweatshirt, eating potato chips and watching some dumb thriller on the VCR, when she could be dressed like a Hollywood starlet and dancing the night away under the admiring glances of scores of handsome men. Mike wanted to stay home. Mike had been willing to go to the ball for Jessica's sake, but now he wasn't. When he found out that Elizabeth wasn't going with Tom but with William White, he changed his mind. Mike said that if he and William White got within five feet of each other, there was bound to be a scene, and he didn't want any more scenes, especially if they involved any member of Jessica's family. "I'm trying to do my best, Jess," he'd said, "but I know I'll lose it if I get near that creep."

Jessica steamed past shelves filled with hair-care products, her eyes on the lookout for the distinctive black-and-silver can that contained

Mike's shaving cream. "Can't you get it into your head that I'm not the frivolous party person I used to be?" she snapped at Isabella.

"You're becoming a zombie instead," Isabella retaliated. "You've been worse than ever since you went back to Mike."

I haven't been worse, Jessica answered Isabella in her mind. *I've been better. I'm taking my marriage seriously. I'm trying really hard to be a better wife, and so far I'm succeeding.*

"I've been busy since I went back to Mike," Jessica said out loud. "That's all, Izzy."

"Busy deciding not to go to the charity ball."

"Busy working on my relationship," Jessica said. All the magazines agreed that was what you had to do with a relationship: work at it. Work very, very hard. Jessica had decided that if she couldn't live without Mike; then she was going to have to learn how to live with him.

Jessica stopped in front of a display labeled SHAVING NEEDS. There were red cans, white cans, blue cans, green cans; there was even a magenta can, but there weren't any black-and-silver ones. Mike was going to have a fit.

Isabella, meanwhile, was staring at Jessica. "Just remember what they say," Isabella said. "All work and no play makes a very dull girl."

Celine swept up the steps of Xavier Hall on the arm of Peter Wilbourne III, as if she were a young queen sweeping up the castle steps to give her humble subjects the honor of an audience. She knew she looked not just beautiful but heartbreakingly beautiful. She'd spent the entire afternoon in the beauty salon and paid a fortune for her magnolia-colored gown. She'd better look heartbreakingly beautiful or someone's head was going to roll.

Celine's smile tightened. Not that someone's head wasn't going to roll anyway. Tom Watts's head was going to make like a bowling ball if she had anything to say about it. She'd come back from an afternoon of having her hair tortured only to find a message from Tom that he wasn't feeling well and couldn't make the ball. "Never mind not feeling well!" she'd screamed at him over the phone. "If you were man enough to tell me in person, I'd kill you."

Peter made some insipid comment about the decorations as they entered the room, and Celine smiled as though he'd said something incredibly intelligent. Thank God for Peter, that was all Celine could say. He'd been so happy that she wasn't mad at him for standing her up the other night, so happy she'd changed her mind about going to the ball with him, that it hadn't even occurred to him to wonder why.

Blessed are the small of brain, thought Celine as the band started up and she stepped into

Peter's arms. *For they will always come running back for more.*

"You're always beautiful, Elizabeth," William whispered as he helped her out of the silver convertible. "But tonight you've done the impossible: you've surpassed yourself."

Elizabeth didn't resist as his lips touched hers. She was feeling beautiful tonight—and unexpectedly happy. Tonight, if only for a few hours, she was determined to forget all her problems and enjoy herself. She was with one of the most desirable men on the SVU campus, and he made her feel like one of its most desirable women. For as long as the music and laughter lasted she was going to forget about Mike, Tom, and every other worry in the world.

"This is going to be a very special evening," William promised as he slipped his arm around her waist and guided her toward the bright lights of Xavier Hall. He gave her a squeeze. "It's not just that I organized the ball and that we've raised a lot of money," he said, his mouth brushing her hair. "It's that I'm sharing it with you, Elizabeth. I hope in the future that we'll be sharing even more."

Determined to enjoy herself, Elizabeth ignored the fact that this announcement didn't really fill her with joy. *It's just because I'm so edgy,* she told herself. *It has more to do with wor-*

rying about Jessica than not caring about William.

Elizabeth hadn't been fooled by the forced cheerfulness in her sister's voice over the phone that afternoon when she'd told her that she and Mike had "decided" not to come to the ball. *She's moved in with that beast again, and he won't even let her out of his den for one night,* Elizabeth thought. *Maybe he'll take apart the living room to entertain her instead.* She frowned, then fixed a smile on her face as William took her elbow just inside the hall.

Elizabeth could feel the eyes follow her and William as they crossed the room to the reserved area of tables where the ball committee was to sit. William must have felt them, too. He pulled her a little closer, his smile pleased. "You know what they're all thinking?" he asked. "They're thinking what a perfect couple we are."

He was making her nervous. William never lacked confidence, but he'd never really talked about them as a couple before. Before he'd been hesitant, even tentative about making any assumptions about how she felt. Now he seemed to be taking how she felt for granted.

"Maybe they're not thinking that at all," Elizabeth answered, her tone purposely light. "Maybe they're just wondering where you bought that incredible suit."

William laughed. "Beauty, brains, and a sense of humor. What more could any man ask for?"

Elizabeth was about to joke that most men she knew wouldn't mind a good cook or an ace pool player when she noticed that William had stopped smiling. He was gazing across the ballroom.

"What's wrong, William?" she asked.

He didn't look over. "Who the hell is that?" he muttered. "What are those kids doing here?"

Bryan's after-school project, Elizabeth thought immediately. *He and Nina really did it. They brought the kids.* She followed William's gaze. Bryan and Nina, dressed for a party if not for a ball, were talking with another couple, and a few feet away were two girls and two boys, looking shy and out of place. One of the boys, Elizabeth noticed, was tapping his foot to the band, but otherwise they looked too terrorized to move.

Suddenly William was unceremoniously shoving Elizabeth toward the table with the engraved card that said *White* on it. "You wait for me here," he ordered, apparently forgetting how dazzled he was by her beauty. "I'll get this straightened out."

Nina caught Elizabeth's eye as William stormed across the room. Elizabeth waved. *I'll wait till Bryan and Nina have straightened William out and then I'll go over and say hello,* she thought.

*   *   *

"Elizabeth. How come you're sitting here all by yourself?"

Elizabeth looked up at the sound of Todd's voice. It was a voice so familiar that she was sure she could recognize it in her sleep.

She gestured to the door, where William, having given up trying to reason with Bryan and Nina, was talking to the dean of students and the security guard. Both the dean and the security guard were shaking their heads. Elizabeth couldn't resist a tiny smile. Not only hadn't William "straightened" things out, but one of the boys, the one who couldn't keep his feet still, had gotten over his shyness and was starting to dance by himself.

"I'm not alone," she said. "I'm with William, but he's busy at the moment."

Todd smiled. It was a smile she remembered from moonlit walks and cozy evenings when they were so comfortable together it was almost like being one person. Out of the corner of her eye she could see Lauren Hill, her red hair braided on top of her head, watching them from the refreshment table.

"I can't believe he's too busy to stay with you," Todd said. "You look beautiful tonight, Elizabeth. Really beautiful."

She felt her cheeks go warm with color. "Thanks, Todd," she mumbled, made awkward not by the compliment but by the sincerity with which he made it. "Lauren looks beautiful, too."

There was so much noise between the music and the dozens and dozens of chatting couples that it was possible Todd hadn't heard her.

"I wanted to thank you for the other day," he said. "It helped just to have you listen."

Elizabeth had the sudden urge to reach out and take his hand. Sitting here with Todd so close and looking at her like that, it was almost possible to imagine them back in high school, back together.

He shifted nervously from one foot to the other. "It's amazing how much better I felt, just talking to you." His gaze went to the floor. "I guess I miss talking to you sometimes."

And sometimes I miss talking to you, she thought, but she checked herself from saying it out loud. Lauren was bearing down on them. She looked as though she had plenty to say.

Winston looked around in a daze as he and Denise entered the gaily decorated hall. It couldn't be true that he, Winston Egbert, failed BMOC and fraternity brother, was really walking with his arm through the arm of the most beautiful woman at the ball. Not only that, but she was laughing at his jokes and brushing against him. He looked over at Denise. Yes, it was true. She really was there, and she really was smiling at him, and she really smelled like ripe mangoes on a balmy summer day. Winston just hoped he didn't faint. He wished he could find some way of really impressing her. If he really impressed her, he might feel confident enough to kiss her at the end of the evening.

Denise shook his arm. "Look at those kids over there, Winnie," she said, pointing to the four of them, dancing by themselves in what were obviously their best clothes. The only people near them were Bryan Nelson and Nina Harper. Everyone else seemed to be keeping their distance. "Where did they come from?"

"Those must be the kids Elizabeth told me Bryan and Nina were bringing with them," Winston explained. "Bryan works with them in some after-school program."

Denise laughed. "He really is too much, isn't he? I bet he figured it would do us good to see the people who are going to benefit from our charity."

"You've got to hand it to Bryan," Winston said. "He never gives up. If someone had attacked me the way they attacked him, I might go for a little lower profile."

Denise nodded. "I might, too," she said, her eyes still on the two girls and two boys. "Man, can they dance," she said, pointing to the smallest boy, who moved so lithely that it didn't seem possible he had bones. "Don't you wish you could dance like that?"

As usual, Winston answered without thinking. "I can dance like that," he said simply.

She turned to him, her eyes so big he was afraid he might drown in them. "You can?"

Winston nodded. "Yeah, I did some camp counseling one summer in high school and the kids at the camp taught me how." He decided to gloss over the weeks of pain and agony it had taken for him to get the hang of it. Or that they'd nicknamed him Leadfoot Winston.

She grabbed him by both shoulders and started shaking him excitedly. "Will you show me, Winnie?" she pleaded. "Will you show me how to dance like that?"

Was the cosmopolitan Denise Waters, looking devastatingly sophisticated in a simple black silk dress and a string of pearls, really asking him to teach her how to rave and break-dance? Winston pinched himself really hard. She was.

"Now?" Winston choked. He pointed to her gown. "But you're all dressed up."

"So what?" Denise grabbed his hand again and started yanking him across the room.

"But Denise," he hissed, "this is a—"

"Dance," Denise said. And then she stopped so suddenly that he slammed right into her. So close he could feel her breath on his cheek. She had brushed her teeth with something minty tonight. "What's the matter, Winnie? Will it embarrass you to dance with those kids?"

Embarrass him? He couldn't imagine doing anything with Denise that could embarrass him. "Of course not. I'd rather dance with them than with most of the other people here. I was just worried . . . about your gown . . ." He was mumbling. He felt numb. It was impossible for him to stand this close to Denise Waters and think of anything but her.

"So you'll teach me how?" she asked.

A voice that couldn't possibly have been his answered her. It was the voice of a guy who'd totally lost his mind. "If you let me kiss you later, I'll show you," this voice said.

Winston stopped breathing, waiting for Denise to either slap him in the face or storm out of the dance, stomping on his foot with her heel before she left.

"I'll kiss you whether you show me or not," she said, her arms encircling his neck. "And why wait till later?"

Jessica set the table with a cloth and candles. At about the time that she imagined Isabella would be taking her shower before the ball, Jessica was whipping up egg whites to make a cheese soufflé to surprise Mike with. At about the time that Isabella was slipping into her dress, Jessica was tossing the salad.

"Mike and I are going to have a better time at home by ourselves than we would at any dumb charity ball," Jessica informed the kitchen as she put a basket of rolls on the table.

At about the time that Danny would be picking up Isabella, Jessica was lighting the candles. She turned off the overhead light. It looked beautiful. Mike was going to be thrilled. She checked the clock. Mike would be home any minute.

Somewhere around the moment when Isabella and Danny stepped into Xavier Hall, Jessica took the soufflé out of the oven. She put it on the table, since according to the recipe there wasn't much else you could do with a soufflé. They didn't reheat well. Jessica checked the clock again. Mike must have been held up by a tricky carburetor or something like that. He'd be home soon.

Jessica sat at the table, watching the candles shrink and the soufflé drop, imagining Isabella dancing with Danny. In her mind she could hear the laughter and mingled voices of a big party, but the only sound in the apartment was the ticking of the clock. Jessica blew out the candles, threw the soufflé away, and decided to do something constructive while she waited for Mike.

She'd been working so hard at being a good wife this week that there wasn't really that much to do. The laundry was done. The apartment was neat and clean.

She walked from the living room to the bedroom, searching for something to keep her mind occupied so she wouldn't start crying.

"I know," she said, feeling like the good wife in a movie. "I'll rearrange the drawers." Mike was always complaining that since she'd moved in and taken most of the dresser, he could never find anything.

Jessica dumped Mike's underwear drawer on the bed. She folded everything, stacking the shorts on one side and the T-shirts on the other. The second drawer was socks. She dumped that on the bed, too, and spent a half hour trying to make pairs. "Maybe he should just wear black socks," she mumbled to herself as she put the drawer back in place. "Then he wouldn't have to worry about losing them."

The third drawer was filled with shirts and sweaters. She dumped that one on the bed.

"Shirts on the left, sweaters on the right," Jessica decided as she began to fold and stack. Her hand touched something hard in the pocket of one of the shirts. Jessica reached in, expecting to find some car part Mike had forgotten about.

But it wasn't. Jessica stared at the black metal object in her hand, hardly able to believe her eyes. She felt a thrill of fear race up her spine. *And where does the gun go?* she wondered numbly. *On the left or the right?*

For a few minutes Jessica just sat there, staring at the gun in her hand, too numb to move or to think. Mike had a gun. What for? Why hadn't he told her? Mike, a man with the temper of a neutron bomb, had a gun. Had he ever used it? Would he ever use it? Would he ever use it on her?

Suddenly, like a dam exploding, Jessica started to cry. All the tension and strain and fear of the past weeks came down on her at once. She'd fallen in love with Mike, and she'd thought that meant that she knew him. But she didn't know him. She had no idea who he was, no idea what he would do. Wiping the tears with her sleeve, Jessica hastily put the gun back in the pocket, flung all the shirts and sweaters back into the drawer, and slammed it into the dresser.

She might not know what Mike would do, but she knew what she had to do. She was going to leave. She'd been lying to herself and lying to him. Tears streaming down her face, she wrote a note for Mike and put it on his plate.

Alexandra Rollins stood at the window of Mark's room, watching the lights from Xavier Hall shining through the night like stars and the beautifully dressed couples floating through its doors.

That should be me, she told herself bitterly. *I should be there with the other Thetas. Why am I being punished? What did I do wrong?*

Behind her, Mark let out a whoop of triumph as the L.A. Lakers scored again. She looked over at him. He was hunkered in front of the television set, a beer beside him, happier than he'd looked in weeks.

"This is a great game," he said, though she had no reason for thinking that he was actually speaking to her. He pointed a pretzel at the screen. "That'll be me in a little while," he said. "Wait'll I get there. Then they're really going to see some shooting."

Against her better judgment, Alexandra found herself walking toward him. "But what about college?" she asked. "You're not saying that you're going to drop out of school?"

He didn't turn around. "I don't think I have to worry about dropping," he said, taking a slug of beer. "I think they're going to dump me like an empty wrapper."

She sat on the arm of the chair he was leaning against. "But you're going to fight, aren't you? You're not going to let them put the blame on you. You should stand up to them."

"What's the point?" He lifted his bottle again. "Maybe they're trying to use me as a scapegoat, but it's not like I was this total innocent. I knew what I was doing." He laughed. "I was happy to do it. I like having money and attention and a nice car and beautiful girls." He raised his beer to the set. "And I'll have them again," he promised himself. "I'll have them again."

And what will I have? Alex wondered as she let herself out of his room.

"Hi, baby, sorry I'm late."

Jessica froze. If only she hadn't stopped to pack a few things at the last minute. If only she hadn't tried to wash away her tears before she left the house. If only Mike hadn't come home just then.

He staggered toward her, his eyes glassy and his smile crooked. "What's the matter?" he demanded, his arms flapping in the air. "Aren't you glad to see me? Aren't you going to kiss me hello?"

"No," she said, amazed to find that her voice still worked. "I'm not going to kiss you hello, Mike." She took a deep breath, trying to decide whether to make a bolt for the door or wait till he was well into the apartment and couldn't try to stop her. When he was like this, he was capable of anything. "I'm leaving you. I've had enough."

He continued to grin. "What?" He kept coming toward her. "What are you talking about, baby? You're not going to leave me. You couldn't. You said you couldn't live without me."

He made a lunge for her and tripped over the overnight bag at her feet, crashing against her.

217

Jessica's heart was racing. "Get off me!" she shrieked, pushing him harder than she'd intended, shouting louder than she'd meant to. She could feel the tears coming again, only this time they were tears of fear. "Get off me, Mike. I'm leaving. That's it." Jessica made a grab for the suitcase, but it flew out of her hand as Mike kicked it with all his might.

"Nowhere!" he roared. "Nowhere, Jess. You're staying right here."

Jessica darted a look at the front door. It wasn't that far away. A few yards, that was all. A few yards and she'd be in the hall. A few more yards and she'd be on the stairs. One flight and she'd be at Steven's. It wasn't far. It couldn't be that hard. She just had to go. Holding back the tears, trying to placate him with a smile, Jessica started edging away.

"We can't go on like this, Mike," she said softly, slowly. "We're driving each other crazy."

He was trying to focus on her, trying to make his words come out the way he wanted them to. "But we love each other," he said, stumbling after her. "We love each other, baby. That's all that matters."

Jessica glanced over her shoulder. She was halfway there. Another four feet and she'd be out.

She kept her voice soft and reasonable. "No, it isn't, honey," she said. "It isn't enough. It—"

He grabbed her so suddenly, he nearly

knocked the wind out of her. "Yes, it is!" he shouted. "It is enough." He started dragging her toward the bedroom. "It is enough!" he bellowed, crying himself from the combination of alcohol and rage. "You'll see, baby, it is enough. You and me, that's all we need."

Jessica pulled back with all her might, trying to grab hold of the furniture as he dragged her through the apartment, but she was no match for him.

"Nobody leaves me!" Mike was yelling now. "Don't you forget it. Nobody, nobody has ever left me." He bumped into the table at the side of the couch, nearly knocking over the lamp.

The lamp. It always worked in the movies.

"You've always thought you were better than me, haven't you?" he ranted on. "You and your snobby friends. What'd you think, Jess? Did you think I was just some kind of toy? Did you think you could just tease me for a while and then go on your merry way? What'd you think it meant when you said you'd stay with me for better or for worse? When you said you'd love me forever? How frigging long is forever where you come from?"

"No!" she screamed back, tears running down her cheeks. "I never thought you were a toy. I meant it when I said I loved you. I did, Mike. You've got to believe that." And she brought the lamp down on him with all her might.

"Where's William?" Nina asked. "I saw you dancing with him before."

Elizabeth pointed to the other side of the hall, where William was dancing with the dean's wife. "Duty called," she explained. "If you move in rich, powerful circles and chair charity balls, apparently you're also expected to dance with the wives of the heads of the college."

"Poor you," Nina said.

Elizabeth laughed. "Actually, I was hoping I'd have a chance to come over here," she said. "This part of the party looks a lot better than the one I'm at."

Nina smiled. What had started out as Nina and Bryan and the four kids, dancing by themselves, had turned into a scene. At least a third of the guests at the ball had come over and were learning how to dance in a way that nobody had ever seen at a gala social event before. Winston and Denise were in the center of the throng, looking as though they were having the time of their lives. Elizabeth had tried to coax William into joining in, earlier, but he'd refused. "I have a reputation to consider, you know," he'd said coolly.

"I think it's been a success," Nina said. She glanced back to where William and the dean's wife were swaying gently. "Except that I don't think William's too happy with us. Pretty much everybody else thinks the kids are great, but he really wanted us to leave." She made a face. "I thought he and Bryan were going to get into a fistfight."

"Bryan doesn't like William very much, huh?" Elizabeth asked, already knowing the answer. Bryan, Tom, and Mike McAllery all didn't like William very much. It was an interesting lineup.

"I think they've had some run-ins in the past," Nina said, obviously trying to spare her feelings. "You know how stubborn Bryan is, and I don't think William's used to being challenged."

"Hey, Elizabeth," Bryan said, suddenly appearing out of the crowd. He grabbed her hand. "How about a dance?"

She tried to pull out of his grasp. "Oh, I couldn't—I don't know—"

Nina gave her a push. "It's easy, Elizabeth. Bryan will show you how."

Elizabeth was just beginning to get the hang of it when a hand grabbed her shoulder from behind. She looked around to find William standing there, his face as blank as a freshly whitewashed wall.

"Come on," he said quietly. "We're going."

Bryan gave her a quizzical look but didn't say anything.

"But the ball isn't over," she protested.

He slipped his arm around her. "I'm really

221

beat, Elizabeth," he said a little more warmly.
"If I stay here, I'll have to dance with every
faculty wife in the school. Let's go back to my
place so I can spend some time with you."

Tom lay on his bed in the dark, staring at
the shadows on the ceiling made by the street-
lights outside. He couldn't face the ball tonight. Not because of Celine, though God
knew there was no such thing as having fun
when Celine was involved. No, the reason he
had dropped out at the last minute was because
of Elizabeth.

Tom closed his eyes. His brain almost hurt,
he'd been thinking so hard, but he forced it to
think some more. What in the world had made
Elizabeth think *he* was the man she was looking
for? All along he'd thought she liked and understood him—maybe not in the way that he would
have wanted, maybe only as a friend and work-
mate—yet all that time she'd suspected him of
running the secret society.

He breathed slowly, trying to concentrate.
No, not all that time. He could almost pinpoint
the moment when things began to change
between them. If only his mind were a television
camera, he'd be able to play back the weeks and
see the first time when she looked at him with a
question in her eyes. He'd make her watch it
with him. "There!" he'd shout. "See that,

Elizabeth? That's when you started having your doubts about me."

Tom's eyes opened. He couldn't pick the exact frame or the exact hour, but he suddenly knew when Elizabeth had started being unsure of him. When William came on the scene. The elegant, the charming, the wealthy, the oh-so-sophisticated, the untouchable William White.

What was it Elizabeth said when he showed her the ring? Tom sat up, concentrating hard. She said, *So it's true*. As if she'd been discussing him with someone else. As though, perhaps, someone else had put the suggestion into her head. Someone like William?

Without realizing he was moving, Tom got off the bed, turned on the light, and pulled his jacket out of the closet, mentally ticking items off a list.

The secret society was national. It had important business connections. Elizabeth had thought Mike McAllery was behind it, at least partly because William had encouraged her to think that. Even though William must have known that Mike wasn't. Mike was outside things like that. He was too much of a renegade. He was one of the few people Tom had ever known who would stand up to anyone—even William White.

Tom put on his jacket as he left the room and started down the corridor. Peter Wilbourne had been at a meeting on Thursday night. And William White had been busy, too. What had he been busy doing? Tom wondered.

By the time Xavier Hall came into sight, Tom was running. He had been blind. He had been blind, stupid, and dense as steel. William White! He'd been standing there, smiling smugly, all the time, and somehow Tom had missed it. William White was the ringleader; he had to be. And if he'd relaxed his harassment of Tom, there could be only one reason. Because he had Elizabeth where he wanted her. He'd alienated her from Tom and had her all to himself now. She wasn't a threat to him anymore. She was a pawn.

He was sprinting now. He was pushing people aside as he ran up the front steps of Xavier Hall.

Tom was vaguely aware that some of the dancers in their suits and fancy dresses were staring at him in horror as he streaked into the room in his sweats and Nikes, but he didn't care.

Jogging through the crowd as best he could, Tom searched for the sight of that golden head. And then he saw Nina. "Nina!" Tom shouted, fighting his way to get within earshot. "Nina, where's Elizabeth?"

If Nina was surprised to see him in his sweat-stained running gear, his eyes wild with worry, she didn't show it. "She went with William," she said quietly.

224

Tom fought to catch his breath. "Where?" he shouted. "Where did they go?"

Bryan was handing him the keys to his car. "My guess is they went to his place."

"Why don't I go get us another drink?" William whispered, pulling gently away from her. "All of this passionate kissing is making me thirsty."

Elizabeth didn't so much answer as breathe a yes. All of this passionate kissing was making her nervous. How had it started? What was she doing in William's apartment? She watched him disappear into the kitchen and sat up, straightening her clothes. She had to get out of here, that was definite. When he came back with the drinks, she'd tell him that she'd had a wonderful evening but that she really had to go.

She stood up. "Where's the bathroom?" she called.

William stood in the doorway. "Through the bedroom, Elizabeth." He smiled. "You can't miss it."

He was right; she couldn't miss it. Elizabeth washed her face and combed through her hair with her fingers.

On her way back to the living room she stopped to look through the books on William's shelves. Austen, Auden, Byron, Cervantes, Chekhov, Dostoyevsky, Eliot, Gogol . . . It was like a library. Between Stein and Stendhal was a leather-bound book with no inscription on the spine.

Almost feeling as though the book were pulling her hand toward it, Elizabeth reached out and took it from the shelf. Thinking it might be very old and valuable, she opened it carefully.

"How weird," she whispered. "It's written in code." From the way the entries fitted together, it looked as though it might be a log of some kind.

"What are you doing, Elizabeth? Don't tell me you got lost?"

Elizabeth looked up, startled. William was standing in the doorway, his eyes on the book in her hand.

"I'm sorry," she said quickly, snapping it shut. "I was just looking to see what you had." She went to push the strange book back in place, but as she did something that had been wedged between its pages fell to the floor.

They both watched it fall as though it were drifting down like a feather.

But it wasn't until it landed that Elizabeth could see what it was. It was a silver bookmark with a broken star carved into the top.

Billie came into the living room with a loaded tray. "Come on, Steven," she said, putting it down on the coffee table. "Let's all calm down,

226

okay? Jessica's been through enough for one night. Why don't you stop cross-examining her for a few minutes and let her have a cup of tea?"

Steven got to his feet and started pacing. "I wasn't cross-examining her," he said defensively. "I was trying to find out the whole story." He shook his head. "I can't believe it, Jess," he said for at least the tenth time. "I can't believe you *married* him. You married that violent, abusive creep—"

"Steven!" Billie glared at him. "Jessica needs a little peace and quiet right now. *Comprende?* Don't start ranting on about it. Give the girl a break."

Steven was muttering now. Muttering and pacing. "I'd like to break the guy's neck."

"Steven!"

Jessica thought Billie was going to throw something at him, her face was so furious. "It—it's all right," Jessica choked out. "I'm all right, Billie, really. I'm just . . . a little upset."

"A little upset!" Steven roared, kicking a stray sneaker out of his way. "A little upset! My baby sister comes running in here, afraid for her life, and she says she's a little upset!"

Billie ignored him. She sat down beside Jessica, stroking back her hair. "You are all right now," she said gently. "You're safe with us." Impulsively she gave Jessica a hug. "Now have some of this herbal tea," she ordered. "It's guaranteed to help shattered nerves."

Steven started pacing again. "I know whose nerves I'd like to shatter," he growled. "When I get my hands on that—"

"Jessicaaa!"

It was like a primal scream. All three of them turned to the front door.

"Jessica! Jessica!"

Jessica's body went rigid with fear. "D-don't let him in here," she begged Billie. "Please, no matter what he says, don't let him in here."

Billie's arm was around her again. "Nobody's letting him in," she promised. "If he doesn't go away, I'll call the cops."

"Jessica!" It was a wail of intense grieving. "Jessica!" He started pounding on the door. "Jessica, you have to let me in!"

"P-please . . . you can't . . ." Jessica was crying now.

Steven started toward the door. "That's it!" he shouted. "It's time he got a chance to pick on somebody his own size."

Jessica's nails dug into Billie's knee. "No!" she screamed. "No, don't open the door!"

Billie was on her feet, too, and heading for the telephone. "Steven! Steven, don't! I'm calling the police."

Steven kept walking as though he hadn't heard them. "I'm not afraid of that punk. You hear me, you cheap hood?" he shouted, his hand on the doorknob. "I'm not afraid of you. You want to fight, then you've got someone to fight. Let's see if you'll push me around the way you push around a defenseless woman."

"Steven, don't!" both Billie and Jessica screamed at the same moment.

Jessica jumped up from the couch, her heart pounding wildly.

But it was too late.

The door swung open and Mike McAllery stumbled into the room, the snub-nosed revolver in his hand.

When Billie saw the gun she screamed.

Jessica was sobbing.

"I want my wife!" Mike shouted. "Get out of my way, Wakefield. I want my wife."

"You can't have her!" Steven shouted back.

As if in slow motion, Steven reached for the gun. He tore it from Mike's grip and it fell to the floor. Both men leapt for it.

"Oh, God, no!" Jessica screamed.

Billie was already dialing 911 when the shot rang out.

Neither of the men on the floor moved. Everything went totally silent for a second that seemed to last for hours.

And then another scream tore apart the night.

We hope you enjoyed reading this book. If you would like to receive further information about available titles in the Bantam series, just write to the following address, with your name and address: Kim Prior, Bantam Books, 61–63 Uxbridge Road, Ealing, London W5 5SA.

If you live in Australia or New Zealand and would like more information about the series, please write to:

Sally Porter
Transworld Publishers
(Australia) Pty Ltd
15–25 Helles Avenue
Moorebank
NSW 2170
AUSTRALIA

Kiri Martin
Transworld Publishers (NZ) Ltd
3 William Pickering Drive
Albany
Auckland
NEW ZEALAND

SWEET VALLEY HIGH ™

Created by Francine Pascal

The top-selling teenage series starring identical twins Jessica and Elizabeth Wakefield and all their friends at Sweet Valley High. One new title every month!

18 PINE STREET

THE PLACE TO BE!

18 PINE STREET is the hot new hangout where Sarah Gordon, her cousin Tasha, Cindy Phillips, Kwame Brown, April Winter, Dave Hunter and Jennifer Wilson meet to talk about their friends, dating – and life at Murphy High.

Look out for the following titles in this great new multicultural series by Walter Dean Myers – available in all good bookshops!